A BODLEY HEAD MONOGRAPH

GENERAL EDITOR: KATHLEEN LINES

A BODLEY HEAD MONOGRAPH

Louisa M. Alcott and the American Family Story

CORNELIA MEIGS

THE BODLEY HEAD
LONDON SYDNEY
TORONTO

ISBN 0370 00801 4
© Cornelia Meigs 1970
Printed and bound in Great Britain for
The Bodley Head Ltd
9 Bow Street, London WC2
by C. Tinling & Co. Ltd, Prescot
Set in Monotype Ehrhardt
First published 1970

CONTENTS

PART ONE
Louisa M. Alcott

1. Fruitlands

It is in an entry in childish writing, set down in Louisa Alcott's diary when she was just eleven, that the story of her life work may be said to have begun. 'Anna and I cried in bed,' she says, 'and I prayed God to keep us all together.'

They were two bewildered children, just beginning to be aware that the unity and happiness of their little family was in mortal peril. The room where they were huddled together in bed was in that draughty old dwelling where a handful of earnest believers had been attempting an experiment in communal living which was now reaching its disastrous and easily predictable end. The low dark-red farmhouse with its attendant rickety barns stood near the small town of Harvard, Massachusetts. This band of hopeful enthusiasts had seen how beautifully the place looked out upon the wide and gracious prospect of woods and meadows and river, with Mount Wachusett lifting green slopes in the distance. It had seemed to them that here was the spot where they could be safe and happy together, to carry out their full ideas for a better world and a higher scheme of living.

Everyone belonging to the community had worked hard, much too hard. They had set themselves the task of cultivating and getting a living out of eleven worn-out acres with no aid from hired helpers or even from horses or oxen to break the stubborn soil with a plough. Spades were thought to be sufficient. Instead of spring the early summer of that year of 1843 was thought to be a practical time for planting.

9

They had concluded that it was wrong to condemn animals to hard labour. Their clothes were linen tunics, for they would not rob the sheep of their covering and they would not use cotton because it was produced by slave labour. They thought it worst of all to eat meat. Yet they were valiantly setting out to establish what Bronson Alcott, Louisa's father, called, 'A new Eden, where man was to live in purity of spirit and in harmony with all living creatures around him.'

Mr Emerson of Concord, Massachusetts, Bronson's closest friend, came to visit them and recorded in his Journal, 'I will not prejudge them successful. They look well in July; we will see them in December.' Louisa's entry in her diary was dated December 10th.

One by one the members of the small company had dropped away and there were left now only Bronson Alcott with his wife Abigail and their four children, and Charles Lane with his young son William. As the harsh New England winter shut down and things began to go badly, each of the two men clung more fiercely to his ideal of what constituted the real purity of living which they had come to seek. Charles Lane was advancing the belief that a man could not live the ideal spiritual life for which they were striving while he was bound by any fleshly ties, that celibacy was essential to a fully preoccupied mind and that if a person were to have the distraction of a wife and family he could not listen truly to the teachings of the inner spirit.

Across the river from the community which they had named Fruitlands was the Shaker settlement which had been there, farming with success, for a long time. It was a community also, the men living in one building, the women in another, with no marriages or families. Shakers were so called by their neighbours from certain motions which attended the forms of their religious ritual. They kept up their numbers through the fact that the government authorities, not having sufficient orphanages, entrusted dependent children to be brought up under their guardianship. The director of the group was a woman, the very able and practical Eldress, who so managed their affairs that they were a thriving organization. Almost every day Bronson and Charles Lane went over to visit the Shakers and discuss their respective beliefs.

Abigail May Alcott, Bronson's wife, always called Abba by her family, watched them go in silence. She was a woman of turbulent and passionate spirit, but she was also practical-minded and self-disciplined enough to see that words were of little use in such a situation. She loved her husband with intense and unquestioning affection. She was silently helpless now as she saw Charles Lane taking him away from her. He was openly urging Bronson to leave his family and cast in his lot with the Shakers. Bronson, conscientious to the innermost depths of his philosophical soul, was wavering as to where his duty could really lie.

Children of ten and twelve, as were Louisa and her older sister Anna, can feel tragedy in the air even if they cannot understand it. On that December night these two were fully aware that some fateful decision was under discussion below them and that upon it depended the whole of their little family's security and happiness. For Louisa, this was one of the most critical moments of her whole life. In it she came to the determination that their household should be defended and kept together at any cost, and that she, the moment she felt herself old enough, was going to see that it was. This resolve coloured everything that she undertook to accomplish through all the years that were before her. It was a resolve that never weakened or faltered or let any other matters come in its way. As we look back through the clarifying perspective of a hundred years, we see that here, indeed, was the beginning of her greatness.

A biographer, entering upon a chosen task, must be able to acquire from the first a full understanding of his appointed central figure. Further, he should learn as much of that person's background as may have contributed to the life which he is in process of writing. Parents are, of course, important factors. But it has to be said of Bronson Alcott, Louisa's father, that a full presentation of him would demand more space than this account can spare, for even after long study of him, from various points of view, he remains a curiously unfathomable man.

His was a figure of real distinction in his own time, although he is someone of whom we are little aware now. He was wise in many things; he was strong and faithful in his principles and his affections; he was generous-minded to more than a fault, sometimes even to a disastrous degree. He was a deep and brilliant thinker and devoted his life to an attempt to establish a true pattern by which man should live and to determine man's relationship to God and to society. Yet he had the possibly immature habit of holding to an emerging theory even to a perilous point and refusing to be shaken from it. Eventually he could rise from the ashes of his mistakes and prepare to go forward again.

He was born on a picturesque and rocky Connecticut

farm where he learned to do the hardest kind of work with all the thoroughness and industry that were ingrained in him. He became well versed in those necessary small skills which farm boys must acquire. Only the scantiest of formal education was available to him, but he was able to bring himself in later years to be accounted a profound scholar and a widely respected philosopher.

From his early boyhood he had been an avid reader and once, very early, a neighbour had lent him John Bunyan's book, *The Pilgrim's Progress*. It took possession of him, as books at that time of a person's life can do, so deeply did it seem to him to touch upon all that he believed in, that symbolic record of a spiritual life so nobly lived and followed to the end. He read it aloud endlessly to his children, who learned to love it and believe in it, especially Louisa. When she came to write *Little Women* many of the chapter headings were titles taken from *The Pilgrim's Progress*, a fact which often puzzles young readers of today who may not have been lucky enough to know good John Bunyan's work.

Forgiveness must be granted to Bronson Alcott, although he made so many mistakes. His real vocation was teaching, for which he had stimulating and inspiring gifts. His special interest was in the teaching of small children, and in methods which have, many of them, been embodied in the educational theory of today. Some of them are, even now, beyond the reach of present-day thinking. His very determination in presenting and living out these educational theories produced again and again questioning, then suspicion, then open hostility. He abandoned his efforts at last, but gave them up without bitterness and pursued his philosophies in other directions and through other means. He made himself responsible for the education of his children but did not seek to do more.

By the grace of God he had a wife who loved him immeasurably and believed in him all her life. Except in moments of extremity, Abba Alcott realized that such a person as he must go his own way. She made no attempt to follow his philosophies; instead she brought her courage and resourcefulness to making what life she could for him and their children. One of Bronson's beliefs, stemming from his conviction that the possession of private property was utterly wrong, was that no man had a right to hire another, or to serve for hire, especially for manual labour. He was a man most personable in appearance, with blond hair, fresh colour, and a continually serene countenance. He had many friends and all bore witness to the fact that he was a most remarkably interesting talker. People can have a gift for conversation as they can have for writing. This last trait he did not possess, but in the realm of talk he was supreme.

When he was a very young man, already knowing that his real vocation was teaching, he made various expeditions through the South, ostensibly in search of a position as tutor in one of the big plantation houses, but actually, to make sure of self-support, with a pedlar's pack of small wares for sale, the necessary conveniences for housekeeping in the country. His personality was always recognized at once and he was often invited to stay several days, given the run of the library with which these prosperous establishments were usually provided, and engaged in serious talk with the master of the house. Book-hungry Bronson made the most of such opportunity and was a guest warmly welcomed by the plantation-owner who was almost always a well-educated gentleman, graduate of William and Mary College or of some English University. Financially, however, these journeys were far from successful, for no one could ever call Bronson Alcott a business man. After falling deeper and deeper into debt every year he finally succeeded in getting a position in a school in Connecticut. It was as a young schoolmaster that Abigail May of Boston first came to know him. They were married there in 1830.

Unfortunately, from the very first, the reception of Bronson's teaching fell into the ever-recurring pattern of approval at first, then slowly-awakening misgiving on the parents' part, then open condemnation. Bronson was obliged to give up school after school, but presently his new ideas came to the notice of a certain Quaker gentleman, Reuben Haines of Germantown, Pennsylvania, who was interested, as many Quakers were, in advancing education. He invited Bronson to join one of the schools which he was hoping to found in his neighbourhood, an offer that was gladly accepted. It was in the comfortable house that Friend Haines had provided for the Alcotts that Louisa was born on November 29th, 1832, a year and a half after her older sister, Anna.

For a little while, life was as it should be with the Alcotts. Abba was of great assistance in the school, which was for very young children. She was the heart and soul of a very happy household. She had the same open-handed generosity as her husband, but in her case it was tempered by a larger and firmer application of common sense. She had a spirited wit and a fine sense of humour that made life merry for them all, and was to do so even in the face of the hard poverty to come.

Abba Alcott has said of herself, and Louisa has mentioned more than once in *Little Women*, that her mother was possessed of a quick temper, controlled only with difficulty, lest it burst out in hot words that were greatly regretted later. Life with the continuously serene Bronson helped to teach her how to control it. To Louisa, who had inherited the same difficulty, she admitted frankly how often she had much ado to hold her impatient spirit in check. She had a notably alert and active mind and she had been given a far better education than Bronson had. She came of a distinguished New England family; one of her relatives, much older than herself, was that Dorothy Quincy who married John Hancock, whose name stands triumphantly at the head of the list of signatories to the Declaration of Independence.

Two years of peace and contentment in Germantown came to an abrupt end. Reuben Haines died suddenly, without having provided for the future of the school which, successful as it was, could not go on without financial support. When the school closed it seemed, after a brief time, to be best for the Alcotts to go back to New England where they would feel more at home, and they therefore made their way to Boston.

Here Bronson had another brief and striking success ending, as before, in disappointment. He founded the Temple School, setting it up in a large room in the Masonic Temple, where tall windows let in the sunshine, where the children had comfortable seats and desks instead of the usually accepted backless benches and where, on the table in the centre, lay a sumptuous copy of Bronson's favourite book, *The Pilgrim's Progress*, for which he had sent to England. The school began to be most favourably talked of; people of the most distinguished families sent their children, and the place had many visitors. On one portentous day there came, among others, a young man of somewhat less than Bronson's age, a former minister in the Unitarian church, now resigned from his place on account of un-orthodox views. His name was Ralph Waldo Emerson. He took immediate measure of Bronson Alcott's true worth and became, with time, such a friend as few men are ever privileged to have.

Growing bolder in the warmth of apparent approval, Bronson Alcott went forward with developing his ideas of proper education, of the study of children's selves and their understanding of the life around them. He published, at his own expense, a little book called *Conversations with Children on the Gospels*. It was greeted with a burst of adverse criti-cism; it was accused of concerning itself with subjects which had no place in young children's comprehension. In the midst of this violent disapproval he went on to publish a second volume which aroused more indignation than the first. It brought about the downfall of the school.

Bronson tried, here and there, to find another place to carry out his theories, but Boston would have none of him. Presently Mr Emerson, with whom he had become better and better acquainted, suggested that he move his family to Concord, a small town on the outskirts of Boston where he would find a healthy place for his children (three of them now), and more congenial company for himself. Ralph Waldo Emerson was beginning to emerge as one of the important thinkers of his day, a time already full of questioning minds and eager seekers after a better way of living. Emerson called it 'The Newness'. The Alcotts took his advice and henceforth, with brief interruptions at different times, were identified with Concord.

Bronson Alcott never taught again, except his own children. He had no hesitation in setting his hand to any kind of work. As his principles did not let him work for actual hire, the arrangement had to be a voluntary exchange on both sides, but he was an extraordinarily good workman and his services were in plenty of demand. He chopped people's winter wood for pay or, if this was not possible, for nothing. He made gardens, for his farmer-boy days had given him a green thumb. He could, when opportunity arose, be a carpenter and builder of neatness and good taste. But such means of support were exhausting and meagre, and the family lived in hard poverty. Although uncomplaining, a man with the mind of a philosopher could well find it deadening. His good friend Mr Emerson could see that this was so.

Some time before, Waldo Emerson had been in uncertain health and failing spirits and had gone abroad to new scenes, new stimulus, new encouragement. He had come back a man restored. This, he was sure, was what his friend needed, and he began to develop a plan. A group of Englishmen had set up an experimental community and an educational project in Kent, not far from London. They had heard of Bronson Alcott's views, and had named their place after him, Alcott House. They had invited him to come over and visit them, and for this Emerson undertook to provide the money. He spoke of raising it among Alcott's friends but later it was revealed that he had provided most of it himself. Bronson Alcott received it gratefully and went.

He came back a few months later full of new plans and ideas. He and his English acquaintances had evolved between them a project for a novel community such as Bronson was certain could prosper in the atmosphere of America. It was to demonstrate how men could come together to live the ideal life, supported by their own labours and uninterrupted by the getting of worldly necessities. There came back with him Charles Lane and his young son. They arrived at Dove Cottage in Concord where Abba and the children were living. She, like the others, caught fire with the idea at once and was as enthusiastic as the rest. The place for their venture was to be bought by Charles Lane, and they finally settled on the old house and farm near Harvard, a situation with a glorious view of beautiful Massachusetts country. A few others came to take part in the experiment and many visitors dropped in to see how it was faring.

Since Bronson Alcott knew all about living on a farm he had some idea of how these worn-out acres would need to be cultivated. It was Charles Lane who insisted that the work should be done without the aid of horses or oxen. He was equally persuasive that they should limit themselves to a vegetable diet. Waldo Emerson came to visit. This development was something that he had not expected and over which he was very dubious. The summer of 1843 went by.

It was Abigail who was disillusioned first. The few other members dropped away, finding the austere living too uncomfortable. Only Charles Lane and his son remained besides the Alcotts. Abba was the only woman to do all the household tasks. Her children helped her but Anna was only twelve and Louisa ten. The youngest was a baby in arms. Louisa helped manfully but she hated housework—then and for the rest of her life. She loved the beautiful country, she delighted in running down the long slopes with the wind in her hair, she looked for berries and wild flowers in the green thickets, but she did not have unlimited time for play when her mother was so overburdened with the work of the house. It was true that their father often prepared the meals and baked the bread, but he also had to labour in the fields. Autumn came, making the view more glorious than ever but bringing chilly nights.

And now, with the prospect of possible failure, arose that question which had been in their minds for weeks. Could pure philosophy be practised when combined with the weight of material encumbrances, or should a man be free to exercise his higher thoughts untrammelled by any bonds? Look at the Shakers and their celibacy! There came, then, that dreadful night when two little girls shivered with dread upstairs while the wills of their elders wrestled together in the room below.

That night Bronson Alcott came to himself. He realized what a desperate wrong he would be doing his family if he succumbed to Lane's arguments. He would not give way. So Charles Lane and his son went across the river to the Shaker settlement, and the harsh New England winter settled down over Fruitlands. But the mental struggle had been too much for Bronson Alcott. He was already worn out by the heavy labour on the reluctant old farm. The ghost of his failure at the Temple School still haunted him. He fell into grievous illness. He did not want to live. For a time it seemed as though the sickness was to be mortal. It was then that Abba Alcott showed the true steel of which she was made. She and her two little girls nursed her husband night and day and in the end the very fact of their loving care penetrated his despair. She began to make arrangements since she knew that they could not spend the winter in the draughty old house. Her brother, the Reverend Samuel May, helped her to what extent he could; she sold her cloak, and her 'silver slice', the last remains of a small cherished hoard of wedding silver. In early January, when Bronson could be moved, a neighbour came up the hill to break a way through the snow with his ox team and took them down to his house. By April Abba had rented a house near the little village of Still River, close by. Bronson worked in the garden as the fresh air and sunshine brought him slowly back to health. Finally they returned to Concord, almost a year after they had left it for ill-starred Fruitlands.

II. Hillside

Concord welcomed the Alcotts back with little comment on the adventure at Fruitlands. The good Hosmers, in whose cottage they had lived before, took them in at once. Abba, however, had made up her mind that the family should now have a settled home. She had received a small legacy from her father and with it she proceeded to buy a house. Her choice, limited by her funds, fell on a rambling brown wooden dwelling on the outskirts of the town, facing the Lexington road, along which the battle of Lexington and Concord had made its way. It was a mere country highway now, lined with stone walls and apple trees. Behind it was a high wooded ridge, a fine place for playing, Louisa decided at once. The price was five hundred dollars more than was available, but this difference was made up by Waldo Emerson. He had a gift for giving without offending people. As Abba had known he would, he took the little family under his wing as soon as they arrived once more in Concord.

For Louisa, her new home held all the charm which she had happily found at first at Fruitlands. From the top of the ridge behind the house one could see far over hills and meadows to the quiet stream of the Concord River. There was one morning when she got up early and climbed the hill to see the sunrise. In the breathless quiet of the dawn she had the sudden feeling, as she looked at the wide beauty of the land, of the nearness of God and the fullness of His presence. It was a moment to be remembered for the whole of her life. It is curious to note that Waldo Emerson records in his Journal having the same experience at much the same place.

He was always at hand to advise or assist where he could, or to discuss philosophy with Bronson, whom he admired and defended when others took occasion to criticize him. Alcott's resolute fashion of pursuing his own way laid him open fairly often to words of adverse comment. There was an incident belonging to this period which Louisa has recorded without date in a letter to a friend. It has been recounted a number of times, but it is so fully illustrative of the Alcotts and their ways that no account of them is complete without it.

One winter night, with snow falling, a neighbour's child came to beg for some firewood, since the baby was sick, the woodbox empty and the father on a spree with all his wages. The Alcotts were low on wood themselves and when Bronson proposed their giving away a generous half, Abba protested, reminding him that they had a baby in the house also. But her husband declared that they should trust in Providence, insisting that 'the weather will moderate or wood will come'. Abba was persuaded to take the risk, so a good share of the wood went to the house of the begging child, with Bronson, one can well suppose, carrying it. Later that night, as the storm grew heavier, a farmer knocked at the door and explained that he had started for town but that the drifts were getting so deep he would like to leave his load of wood there and they could pay for it at their convenience. It was not often, however, that Bronson's hopeful generosity was so directly justified.

The house, called by the Alcotts 'Hillside', had been long unoccupied and was in great need of repair. This Bronson sturdily set himself to accomplish. His skill and taste made the old house respectable and comfortable, as well as attractive. He laid out a charming garden for which there was ample room. Neighbouring housewives who had raised their eyebrows over the fact that Bronson Alcott would not work for hire even to support his family were appeased now when they saw how he toiled to make habitable and pleasant the house and the land around it.

The four years that the Alcotts spent there, 1845 to 1849, were, as we can now see, a most significant time in Louisa's life. As she grew into adolescence, she was extremely happy, her mind teeming with plans and purposes. She wanted one thing more, however. She kept saying to her mother, 'If I only had a little room of my own, where I could be alone.'

Her father agreed that it might be managed. Beside the big barn there was a small shed for which there seemed to be no use. He sawed it in two and attached the halves as small wings at each end of the house. One was Louisa's little room. She was enchanted with it. There was an outside door so that she could slip away into the garden whenever she wanted. No one objected even when she stole out at night to climb into the old apple tree and watch the moon mount the sky until, as she admitted, 'the owls scared her to bed'.

Mr Emerson had given her the run of his library, where she spent hours of delight. He was a great admirer of the German author Goethe whose ideas and writings were in the ascendant at that time. Louisa found on his shelves the English translation of *Goethe's Correspondence With a Child*

and took it home with her. The 'child' in question was
Bettine Brentano, who had conceived a hero-worshipping
affection for the famous poet and poured out her strikingly
immature soul in a series of exuberant letters to him.

Goethe's answers were brief and non-committal but
always appreciative. That he attached value to the letters
was proved by his having kept them all. Bettine, who was,
in fact, twenty-two years old when she first met Goethe and
therefore scarcely the child that she professed to be, had
become by her marriage Bettine von Arnim. After Goethe's
death she secured the letters and published them, with his
replies, under the somewhat misleading title which so
captured Louisa's fancy. Louisa decided that it would be
interesting and romantic to be like Bettine and chose Mr
Emerson for the object of her admiration. She wrote profuse
letters, pouring out a young spirit which was most unlike
Bettine's. She has called those years of her growing up 'The
Sentimental Period', but it is characteristic of her innate
good sense that she destroyed the letters before anyone,
certainly not Emerson, could see them. Although even with
effort she could not imitate the so-called child Bettine, the
influence of her letters left in Louisa's mind a taste for
gothic romance which showed its effect later. She also came
upon the tales of the French writer La Motte Fouqué,
Undine and *Sintram and his Companions*. In *Little Women*
we find Jo carrying a book of his stories in her pocket as a
cherished Christmas gift.

During this time the long-empty barn came into full use
as the home of a busy and interesting amateur theatre. Thus
the first of Louisa's writings were not the short stories
which first found publication but a series of lurid dramatic

compositions in which she was sometimes assisted by her sister Anna. This older sister had real talent as an actress; she became also a skilled stage carpenter who stopped at nothing in achieving impressive, although sometimes collapsible, stage effects. Many years later the manuscripts of these dramatic effusions came to light. They were edited by Anna and published under the discerning title *Comic Tragedies*. The names alone give full revelation of their kind and quality: 'Norma, Or The Witch's Curse', 'The Captive of Castile, Or The Moorish Maiden's Vow'. Scenery and costumes were of the most ambitious sort.

The writer of this monograph had no need, in this case, to go into extensive research, for she knew the plays well and appeared in two of them in her own family's theatricals. Once at the age of eight she 'walked on' as a page-boy bearing the cup of wine into which the villain pours the fatal poison; later at the maturing age of eleven, she assayed the title role in 'The Unloved Wife, Or Woman's Faith'. What would childhood be if it did not have its capacity for illusion? It is to be noted that, in spite of their absurdity, the situations in these plays are based on the influence of character on character and not on accidental circumstance. The leading figures had no more than one characteristic apiece, but that was really enough to tell them apart. In so young an author this can be recognized as instinctive talent, not deliberate intention.

All this marked the happy side of the four years at Hillside; there was, unfortunately, another aspect of the Alcotts' life there. Ways of earning a livelihood in Concord were few. Abba had done all she could by sewing, but this was far from being enough for a household of six, for there were now two more girls: Elizabeth, born during the Temple School period, and May, who was carried to Fruitlands as a baby. Waldo Emerson did all that he could, but he was not a man of great means. He offered, rather rashly at this time, to take the whole family into his household, but this Abba Alcott, even in her extremity, had the good sense to decline. Yet something had to be done to keep shoes on their feet and food on the table. The Alcotts were virtually penniless.

In her despair Abba admitted all this to a friend who came to see her, Lydia Maria Child. It was she who suggested that it might be wise to move to Boston where she felt sure that through her influence she could find Abba a salaried position. Could they make up their minds to go? It was a difficult question to decide. Louisa had set up a little school in the barn, with the scholars mostly composed of the Emerson children, but it brought in little money. And could they bear to leave their Concord friends? Bronson had made a warm acquaintance with a neighbour living further out of town than they did; he was Henry David Thoreau. Like Emerson and Bronson he was a philosopher, a man deeply interested in birds and plants and animals, and drawing fundamental truths from the study of them. He had built himself a hut on the shores of Walden Pond. He busied himself, besides, with writing books that got very little recognition when they were published but in due time were hailed as classics. Bronson spent most Sunday afternoons discussing philosophical matters with him. And there was Waldo Emerson. How could they possibly get on without him? But he came often to Boston; they would not be out of reach of his advice, companionship and help. Lydia Maria Child sent word that Abba could have a position with a charitable society for visiting and investigating. They said goodbye to Hillside, put it up for sale and took their way to the city.

It developed now that Bronson had been laying a plan for an activity of his own, the setting up of a series of talks, similar to, but not too closely resembling, the lectures for which Emerson was now growing famous. The Alcotts took a house on Atkinson Street, and Bronson rented a room close to the bookshop of Elizabeth Peabody who had been Bronson's assistant in the Temple School days. Her bookshop had become a sort of Mermaid's Tavern meeting place, where many of the philosophical, ministerial and other intellectuals were prone to gather. In the room that he had rented Bronson Alcott now began to conduct the first of a series of what he called Conversations, meetings like those of the philosophers of old, carried on by talk, by question and answer and discussion. There was, at this beginning, little money in such an undertaking, particularly since Bronson was apt to invite people to attend free if he had any doubt of their ability to pay the very small fee that was involved. Anna was teaching; Abba's work was onerous and her salary small, but it was enough to keep the family together.

The first summer of their stay in Boston was most unpropitious. Abba, receiving some poor emigrants newly arrived, let them come to eat their lunch in the small garden of the house where the Alcotts had settled, to give them a place of refuge until she could find work and housing for them. They went away but they left smallpox behind them. The whole family had it, the girls lightly, the father and mother with great severity. 'No one came near us,' Louisa records. They did not even have a doctor. Mercifully they all recovered satisfactorily.

Louisa, now seventeen, helped Anna with her teaching, but she was never happy in a teacher's role. She was fond of children and understood them, but she was impatient of laggards, and, having herself been taught by Bronson's unorthodox methods, never quite knew how to adapt herself to the accepted school routine. She had written a little book of stories for Ellen Emerson, *Flower Fables*, which she brought to Boston hoping to find a publisher, but failing in that, she sought something else that would help the family finances.

Her mother had opened an employment office, in connection with her duties as what we now call a social worker. There arrived one day a gentleman who said that his invalid sister was in need of a 'companion' who might be asked to do a little light housework but who was to be treated with the utmost respect and consideration. Louisa, hearing the conversation, suggested, after he was gone, that she might apply for the place. Her mother was dubious but finally, since no one else seemed suitable, Louisa offered herself and was immediately accepted.

She found that she was expected to do the hardest kind of drudgery, chopping the kindling, carrying heavy burdens up long flights of stairs, cleaning and scrubbing. As the days went by she was paid nothing, and at the end of a month she realized how shamelessly she was being exploited, and declared that she was going to leave. The invalid sister wept copiously at the idea, as well she might, and soft-hearted Louisa consented to stay until someone else could be found. Mrs Alcott, however, refused to recommend anyone else to such a place and after two weeks more Louisa departed. She was given a small purse which was supposed to contain her wages. When she got a little distance from the house she opened it to find that it contained four dollars. She could have wept with disappointment, but her indignation was stronger still. When she got home her father insisted that the money was to be returned, as a payment that was beneath contempt. It went back, therefore, and, it is to be hoped, brought a proper sense of humiliation to the gentleman who had made the arrangement.

After this, in desperation, Louisa opened a small school of her own, in the parlour of their house. She liked teaching no more than before, but it was the only way for a young woman to earn money. She supplemented it by sewing, in which she was happily and creatively adept. Anna was teaching now in an institute for retarded children in Syracuse—a position for which her uncle, Samuel May, who had a church there, had recommended her. Three years passed and then a great event occurred. Louisa's first story was published—in 1852.

She has not left us a record even of its name and she speaks of it very nonchalantly in a letter to Anna. 'I sent a little tale to the *Gazette*, and Clapp asked H.W. if five dollars would be enough. Cousin H. said yes and gave it to me and a nice parcel of paper, saying in his funny way "Now Lu, the door is open, go in and win."' It was advice earnestly and literally taken. She had always been scribbling stories, a work to which she now bent herself with renewed and encouraged energy. She found a publisher, George Briggs, for *Flower Fables* which appeared in 1855.

There was an incident during this residence in Boston which Louisa describes in full detail in her Journal. Her father's plans for Conversations had gradually enlarged and, under Emerson's advice, he had undertaken a trip to the West where opportunities seemed to be opening. He came home one winter night, tired, hungry, cold and disappointed. He was warmly embraced and fed and made much of, and not until everything possible had been done for his comfort was he asked the question which was in everyone's mind. May spoke it: 'Well, did people pay you?' He opened a thin purse and took out a single dollar. He told them, 'Many promises were not kept, but I have opened the way and another year shall do better. My overcoat was stolen and I had to buy a shawl.' There was a little pause then Abigail said, 'I call that doing *very well*. Since you are safely home, dear, we don't ask for anything more.'

In the summer of 1855 Louisa was invited to spend some weeks in Walpole, New Hampshire, where the cousin to whom she always refers as L.W. (Lizzie Wells) was staying. The change of air and scene did her much good after all the noise and dirt of city life. She realized that her family needed something of the same sort of change and persuaded them to come to spend the winter in Walpole where they had been offered a small house, rent free. There were dramatics in the barn as in the old days at Hillside, and Bronson held some of his Conversations in nearby towns. But by November Louisa had made up her mind to embark on a venture of her own, to return to Boston and support herself, and thus ease the family situation. It would be the first real step in that plan for taking care of them which she had formed so early and with such determination. She had written another little book, *Christmas Elves*, to the same pattern as *Flower Fables*, and with this and the manuscripts of further tales in her little trunk she rolled away in the clumsy stage-coach, full of ideas and with all the hope in the world.

III. Orchard House

It is pleasant to know that Louisa's hopes, modest indeed, although at moments very wide in extent, began almost at once to win equally modest fulfilment. All she really wanted was to be able to support herself and have a surplus, no matter how small, to send back to her family in Walpole. She found some tutoring to do for the little invalid daughter of a friend. This would pay her three dollars a week which would cover the price of her board and room, with fire, in a comfortable boarding house managed by a friend of the family on Chauncey Street. A 'sky parlour', Louisa dubbed it, with little elbow room, but here she could sew without interruption, her needle flying, and 'simmer her stories', to scribble them down on Sundays. There seemed to be plenty of sewing assignments to be found in that age when sewing machines were not yet in circulation. She could look back with satisfaction on her one story in the *Gazette* and on what she termed 'the principal event of the last winter', the appearance of her small book *Flower Fables*. She had been able to put it into her mother's Christmas stocking with a little note which said, 'I hope to pass in time from fairies and fables to men and realities.' She distinctly knew whither she meant to go. She admitted cheerfully that, for the time being, sewing paid her better than writing. The rate of payment can be calculated from the figures she gives for her receipts for one sewing task: 'a dozen sheets, a dozen

C

pillowcases, six fine cambric neckties and two dozen hand-
kerchiefs', which she had to stay up all night to finish. The
return was four dollars.

Her mind was continuously on her family in the advancing New England winter in New Hampshire. The autumns
in New England are strangely glorious, but the winter is
something else. Were they comfortable and happy? Were
they well? All news from them was cheerful until the winter
had passed. In June she was called to Walpole for an
unhappy emergency.

Abba Alcott, indefatigable in her pursuit of good works,
came across a family in Walpole living in a filthy and miser-
able dwelling which their landlord refused to clean up until
Mrs Alcott threatened to bring an action against him for
maintaining a public nuisance. Various members of the
family had fallen ill with scarlet fever and two children had
died. Abba nursed them bravely, and then, to her terrified
dismay, found that she had carried the infection home to
her own children. Elizabeth and May were both very ill,
Elizabeth the most seriously. Louisa helped with the nursing and saw vigorous young May restored to full health.
Elizabeth came back to a semblance of wellbeing, but never
to her former strength. Louisa remained at Walpole all
summer helping to nurse her. The tie between these two
was very close, and Elizabeth grew to depend greatly on her,
for it was plain that Louisa was as good a nurse as she was a
needlewoman. In the autumn, however, when her sister
seemed to be definitely improved, Louisa returned to
Boston. The need for money was more pressing than ever
and there was little chance of earning in Walpole. It was
with an anxious spirit and with no excited hopes that she

said goodbye to them all in November when she once more was ready to set her hand to any work that she might find.

But this time things were not easy. Mr Clapp, who had taken her first story, thought that he could guarantee her ten dollars if she could continue supplying him with more. But the little invalid whom she had hoped to tutor seemed now well enough to go to school, so that source of income was no more. Yet at the moment when Louisa scarcely knew whither to turn, the arrangement of teaching small Alice was renewed. She had been prepared to take a place 'to sew ten hours a day at a Girls' Reform School, to make and mend' but the new offer spared her this.

She had made acquaintance with Theodore Parker and his kindly, pleasant wife. Parker was a distinguished leader in the religious and political thought of his time. Like Emerson, he was a Unitarian minister of unorthodox views, but unlike Waldo Emerson he had still retained his place in a prominent Boston church. Louisa went often to hear him preach and got both inspiration and strength from his sermons. He was a man of energetic and fearless spirit, a supporter of Abolition in a city where there was much pro-slavery feeling. He was one of those who secretly assisted runaway slaves to escape northward to freedom in Canada, as earnest in that cause even as Bronson or Abba or Abba's brother Samuel May in Syracuse. One of Louisa's earliest memories was of opening the door of the brick oven—perhaps in the first cottage in Concord, perhaps at Fruitlands, we do not know which—and of seeing a dark face peer out at her. She ran away in childish terror and later she was told to say nothing about it, nothing to anyone, ever. Theodore Parker, it is said, kept a loaded revolver in the drawer of his desk in his minister's study, to protect any of his hidden guests if the law came to claim them. One of Parker's close friends was William Lloyd Garrison who was once seized by a mob and dragged through the streets with a rope around his neck. Feeling between North and South was rising very high, and in propertied Boston the weight of public opinion at that time supported slavery. The police managed to rescue Garrison from the crowd, but for safety they had to take him into custody at the Town Hall. The first people to visit him were Bronson and Abba Alcott, just 'to show Boston where we stood', as they declared.

On Sunday evenings the Parkers kept open house to all who cared to come and thither Louisa went regularly, tall, shy and prone to remain sitting quietly in a corner. Inwardly she glowed with excitement and pleasure at seeing all the great persons there. For her, stories were coming forth in a steady stream, with increasing returns as she came to be better known. She always knew instantly how to spend any money left over after her needs were satisfied—on shirts for her father, boots for her mother, a new hat for May. Her contribution was beginning to be a real item in the family budget, to her intense satisfaction. She also records with jubilation the possession of her 'first new silk dress' given her by her cousin Lizzie Wells in which she went to two parties on New Year's Eve, feeling 'as if all the Hancocks and Quincys beheld me'.

Another summer at Walpole passed and in October it was clear that it was time for the Alcotts to move again. Nathaniel Hawthorne, now appreciated as one of America's great novelists, had bought Hillside, renamed Wayside, and was living there with his family, enjoying the results of Bronson's excellent handiwork. Abba Alcott, with determined thrift, had managed, even in extremity, to segregate the money received for it and, thanks to Louisa's help, had not encroached upon it. They had all missed Concord and Waldo Emerson's companionship and helpful friendship, Bronson in particular feeling the need for the intellectual stimulus of his philosopher friends in Concord. It was unhappily plain that with Elizabeth's failing health, another winter in the Walpole snowbanks would be most unwise. They returned to Concord, having bought the old house next to Hillside, below the same wooded ridge and somewhat nearer to where the Emersons lived.

Again and again they had set up housekeeping in a new place, but had never, any one of them, lost the sense of home. Family loyalty, an unshakable belief in family solidarity, a never-failing abundance of family love had gone with them always, had rescued them from disaster in the crisis of Louisa's childhood at Fruitlands. And, as we shall see, it was the rock and foundation upon which Louisa's genius was built.

The move to Concord was made in October of 1857. While Abba took Elizabeth to Boston for medical advice, Anna and Louisa, along with Bronson, set about the Herculean task of making the house ready. They had rented some rooms in a place in Concord where Elizabeth could be made comfortable, until the final preparations were complete. Hillside had been in need of repair, but this was four times worse. The owner had frankly declared that the building was of no use except for firewood and 'threw it in' with the purchase of the land. But like Hillside, it was

basically a sturdy old dwelling, and the vigorous resourcefulness of the Alcotts did wonders with it. As their hands
renewed it, it still stands today, hospitable and comfortable,
a hundred years afterwards. While Bronson sawed and
hammered, the girls planned closets, arranged bedrooms,
contrived places for books. Bronson, who had sold the
whole of his library to pay the debts incurred by the Temple
School, could now amass another. A portion of the low-
ceilinged attic was to be Louisa's writing place (one could
scarcely call it a study). May painted a motto to be hung
over the fireplace in the library. It had been composed by
Bronson's friend Channing:

'The hills are reared, the valleys scooped in vain,
If Learning's altars vanish from the plain.'

Through all their struggles with dirt and cold, their
main thought was of Elizabeth: how to make a place where
she could be comfortable and happy, if only for a little
time. But she was never to live there. She died in March
1858, before they were ready. Through the last days of
Louisa's close and devoted nursing the sight of her sister's
patient courage set a stamp on Louisa's turbulent spirit
which was to last through her life. Trouble she had known
in plenty. Of grief this was her first experience, and it
struck very deeply. A month later, while she was still in
Concord, Anna came in after visiting the Pratt family, who
had been friends of the Alcotts since the Fruitlands days.
She announced that she was engaged to the son of the house,
John Pratt. Louisa took the news badly. Here was her
family, for whom she had cherished such hopes and ambitions, whom she had been so determined to keep together,

melting away before her eyes! She did not realize that in her devoted nursing of Elizabeth she had done more for her than any money could ever do. 'I feel strong when you are there,' Elizabeth had once told her. Nor could Louisa know that her time of great service to Anna was still to come.

At the end of the summer she went once more to Boston, for the problem of money was still acute. She had fallen so deeply into sorrow and despair that, one day before she left, as she walked along the mill dam she thought how simple it would be to let death settle all her worries and disappointments. But her spirit rallied and she carried away to Boston the resolve, recorded in her Journal, 'to take Fate by the throat and shake a living out of her'.

It may not have been the best approach to the task before her, for certainly luck now deserted her. Employment, even sewing, seemed very difficult to find. She began to think of nursing as a way to make a living, since all her family commended her ability in a sickroom. 'I may try it yet,' she told herself darkly.

In this time of bewilderment, sorrow and disappointment, two friends were of immense help to her. Theodore and Mrs Parker were deeply interested in her and were aware of the depths through which she was passing. He by his public preaching, she by kindly advice in woman-to-woman talks gave her much aid in gathering new strength. She has said that the people who contributed most to her education were Waldo Emerson and Theodore Parker, Emerson in the enlargement of her intellectual horizon, Parker in teaching her how to live courageously in the face of sorrow and bitterness.

There was one Sunday morning when she was at the lowest level of her spirits and her hopes. As happens occasionally to those in need of spiritual restoration, she heard Theodore Parker preach a sermon which seemed composed for her alone. It chanced to be on 'Laborious Young Women' and he had evidently had Louisa and many others like her in mind as he composed it.

'Trust your fellow-beings,' he said, 'and let them help you . . . Accept the humblest work until you can find the task that you want.' She was to put his advice to the severest test and, in the end, to find that he counselled truly.

It was no great wonder, as she faced one disappointment after another, that she allowed a secret longing to come to the forefront of her mind. Ever since the dramatics in the Hillside barn she had found the idea of being a successful actress an alluring vision. She had definite ability, although not so much as Anna. Through friends she was now offered by a Mr Barry, a manager, the opportunity for a try-out in a real performance on a real stage. The matter was to be a profound secret until the great day. But Mr Barry broke his leg and could not put on the projected play, and somehow the plan leaked out and came to the ears of certain members of the May clan. 'It would not do. No, it would never do at all,' they declared with one voice, a chorus of Sewalls and Warrens and Quincys. In the end, on her mother's advice, Louisa reluctantly abandoned the cherished plan. She finally had to admit to herself that the life would be as hard as the one she had, with the rewards perhaps equally uncertain. She toyed with the idea of writing for the stage and she did compose one play and also a farce. The farce, with the help of friends, did finally come to a performance but has since been forgotten. And the play never saw the light of day. Yet her interest in things dramatic remained always with her.

She turned once more to the writing of stories but, rather surprisingly, in an unexpected direction.

Certain tales that she had dashed off in haste, under the need for money, had found special favour with certain editors. The public fancy at that moment was for the ultra-romantic which was often very badly done, since such literature has to be extraordinarily well done to be worth anything at all. Certain editors found that Louisa, with her gift of ready inventiveness, could produce, in easy quantity, just such tales that would please their readers who were developing an appetite for a lurid and romantic style. Clapp, the editor of the *Gazette*, the first paper to accept a contribution from her, said he would take all that she could bring him. Loring, a Boston publisher, was equally receptive. Louisa quotes him in her Journal as saying that her tales were 'so dramatic, so vivid and full of plot' that they were just what he wanted. Since, as she declares, they took only a little time to write, she fell into the habit of producing more and more of them. In later years she never allowed them to be republished, except for one, 'A Whisper in the Dark', to satisfy the curiosity of young readers as to what Jo March's 'necessity stories' were really like.

She had far too innocent and unsophisticated a mind for the tales to be degraded or sordid, but they were all luridly impossible, set against backgrounds totally unknown to either the author or the reader. Some titles, cited in *Little Women*, indicate what they were like: 'A Phantom Hand',

'The Duke's Daughter', 'The Curse of the Coventries'. She carried out her effects by using witches, hobgoblins and ghosts. Her youthful mind had delighted in *The Mysteries of Udolpho* and tales of Undine and Sintram. Behind it all was the unfortunate example of Bettine von Arnim, and her gushing letters to Goethe. Louisa was well aware that she was not doing the best that was in her, but the desire to help her family overrode any qualms.

Even where far-fetched romance did not prevail, there was also at this time a fine taste everywhere for sentimentality, the most insistent fashion of that day. Sentiment itself belongs to real life; sentimentality is something far different. A writer can convey sentiment by action, but not so with sentimentality. It has to be conveyed by words alone, empty words, for it is a totally artificial emotion. During this period Louisa even fell into that error also, but not to such excess as other writers of her time. But in her hasty output she failed to grasp the fact that real creation must be based on living and genuine experience.

The new home in Concord had been named Orchard House and here Anna was married in May of the year after Elizabeth's death. It was a very simple ceremony, conducted by the girl's uncle, Samuel May, to whom they were all devoted. After it was over, when Anna and her new husband stood under the magnificent elm tree outside the door, the guests joined hands and danced around them, dispelling completely any sense of sorrowful parting. They were to live not far away, in a little house which Louisa christened the Dovecot. She has described the wedding journey as being Anna's quiet walk with her husband from one home to the other. Louisa had recovered from her sense of deprivation in Anna's marriage and rejoiced over her sister's happiness.

Through the influence of Waldo Emerson, Bronson Alcott had been made superintendent of the Concord public schools with a salary of one hundred dollars a year. He had learned by now to be less uncompromising in his urge to have his theories on education accepted, even when he knew that he was right. He did much for the schools and at the end of the year issued a report which was widely read and approved as it would not have been in earlier years. At the end of the term he held a festival of children, for which Louisa wrote a song. At its conclusion there was an un-rehearsed incident. A tall handsome boy stepped forward and presented their principal with a copy of *The Pilgrim's Progress* 'from the children of Concord'. The loss of that fine copy which had been sold to pay the debts of the Temple School could not be other than a bitter memory. Such recollection was now swept into oblivion, for the greatness of their schoolmaster had been recognized at last.

Louisa remained in Concord throughout the summer that followed Anna's wedding. She had no need to go to Boston to look for employment; she could earn more money by writing than by any other activity and she could write at home. She declared a moratorium on romantic tales; her creative mind had turned itself in another direction. She was at work on a novel, her first one, which she was to call *Moods*. She toiled over it early and late, for as she said, it simply had to be written.

She came to the end of it finally and put it aside 'to settle', for she had no idea of its real worth. She was immediately off on another which, in the making, she called

Work but afterwards renamed *Success*. This she did not entirely finish. The Civil War had begun and the guns of Fort Sumpter had sounded throughout the land. All women, Louisa most definitely included, were sewing or knitting or rolling bandages or scraping lint for 'our boys'.

Early in 1862 Elizabeth Peabody, that lady of many projects, became interested in opening a kindergarten in Boston which would present to Americans the new ideas of the Swiss educator, Pestalozzi. She was determined that Louisa should be the head of it, and since Miss Peabody was used to getting her own way, Louisa reluctantly consented, and returned to Boston. The venture was not a fortunate one. To make the experiment cover as wide a field as possible, Elizabeth Peabody took in a rashly large number of pupils who could not afford to pay. The result was disastrous to the school's finances since the fees could not cover a living wage for the teachers, so it was arranged that they should stay, in turn, at the houses of different parents, a revival of the old country custom of the teachers 'boarding around'. For proud and independent Louisa it was a singularly inappropriate expedient and she suffered deeply under it. Her record in her Journal speaks for itself: 'I never knew before what insolent things a hostess can do nor what false positions poverty can push one into.' By spring she decided that she would endure it no more and arranged to travel to Concord every day so that she could 'have my dear people at night and not be a beggar'. By the last month she refused to return at all and May took her place so that her promises would be fulfilled. She was now done with teaching for ever.

She was certainly not content with the kind of stories she had been writing for editors only too avid to accept them.

She was not sure of the quality of her two novels, one unfinished. The heavy campaigns of the war had begun and voices were crying out everywhere for nurses to work in the army hospitals. She had another vocation besides writing; she had once thought of pursuing it altogether. It was time to follow it now. In November 1862 she volunteered as a nurse for hospital work in Washington.

IV. Georgetown Hospital

When Southern influence in the Congress of 1850 succeeded in passing the Fugitive Slave Law it was hailed as a great political victory for the States of the South. It was, instead, a disaster leading indeed to a future victory, but not for the cause it was intended to serve. Up to that point any State where slavery was forbidden was free ground so that a slave, once reaching it, could not legally be taken back. Thus, when Harriet Beecher Stowe was projecting in her mind the writing of *Uncle Tom's Cabin* she could envisage that dramatic moment when Eliza, with her baby in her arms, crossed the Ohio River on the breaking ice to safety. No one can forget the thrilling suspense of that imaginary scene, certainly no one who has experienced the breaking of ice in a great river. It does not give way little by little, but sweeps down all at once, with a great crashing and grinding and rearing on end of huge blocks of ice, yellow with the mud of the bottom. But once ashore, Eliza and her baby were free.

The new law, however, altered all that. There were dire penalties for those who broke it and helped runaway slaves to escape to Canada, the nearest region where slavery was fully prohibited. The ruling transformed the whole citizenry of the United States into accessories to an abuse which so far they had been willing to suffer without interference but which nearly the whole of the North was furiously unwilling to support. A law which three-quarters of a nation considers unjust is impossible to enforce. The penalties for breaking it were harsh; a man caught slave-running could be fined to the extent of losing his whole property; there were bounties offered for information which would incriminate those who were helping the runaways. But hundreds of people broke the law; in great part they were among the foremost citizens, leaders in their own area of society. As was inevitable in such a situation racketeering sprang up wherever there were scoundrels who were willing to make money by giving information. Slaves escaped, not in smaller numbers, but in greater, in hundreds and then thousands. The South complained bitterly that its whole economic structure was threatened. If there *had* been any hope of settling the difficult problem of slavery and Secession it was gone and war, though slow in coming, was now inevitable.

Louisa had given up the lurid stories and had been possessed by the writing of her two novels, 'falling into a vortex' over them, as she liked to express it. The editors upon whom she had relied for acceptance were somewhat doubtful, for they had become accustomed to looking to her for something very different. Both books were published and both have been forgotten.

Any young writer, discouraged over his own first efforts, disheartened by rejections, uncertain of his own powers, would do well, for his education, to read Nathaniel Hawthorne's first novel *Fanshawe*. In it he was only feeling his way towards a style of his own and the building of a plot. It is distinctly poor in its field, but it was soon followed by a work of another atmosphere and an achievement of true genius, *The Scarlet Letter*. The Hawthornes and Alcotts were next-door neighbours now and close friends, and although there is no record of Louisa's having read *Fanshawe*, it seems likely that she did.

Even in the midst of all this writing she was very faithful in taking part in all the war work that was going on among the women of Concord. She was good company at the work tables and immensely capable with her needle. But this was not enough for her. 'The blood of the Mays is up!' Her grandfather had been an army officer and she felt herself to be a 'fighting May'.

Louisa had many times wished she were a boy; she wished it doubly now, but she could make the best of being a girl. There were plenty of women to sew and roll bandages, but finding enough nurses was a different matter. There were no training schools then; one learned to nurse through natural aptitude and hard experience. All who knew Louisa well agreed that she was a remarkable nurse. The impatience which, as a teacher, she found hard to control did not manifest itself when she was in a sickroom. She could not bear to see careless children so indifferent to the priceless gift of education, but people who were ill and suffering enlisted her pity at once. Her sympathetic spirit and her interest in people—all people—made for success in this field as well as in that of writing. She had learned to be deft and skilful in the duties of a sickroom through the months of Elizabeth's long illness and through her mother's occasional breakdowns, which Abba cheerfully described as 'the irrepressible conflict between sickness and the May constitution'.

She went through a flurry of hasty preparation with high expectation of she knew not what. There was a moment of doubt at the last. She was aware that she was taking her life in her hands—she did very nearly lose it. But her mother encouraged her through the last moment of indecision; her father, who was too old to go, said he was giving 'his only son'. For most of one breathless day she hurried about Boston for passes, a few purchases, some goodbyes; then she climbed aboard the absurdly inadequate train and went rolling away southward.

She had travelled very little and had never seen, since she was a baby, any city other than Boston. She arrived in Washington after many changes, from train to boat and back to train again. She made her way to the Union hospital, to which she had been assigned, in Georgetown just outside the city. Even at first glance, and certainly in the first hours, her efficient eye took note of the dirt of the old building which had once been a hotel, saw the confusion and in-efficiency with which a totally unprepared organization was attempting to meet the overwhelming tasks that the war was bringing in, daily and hourly. Her heart did not sink; this was a challenge.

She says of herself that she was ignorant, awkward and bashful at first but the men made no complaint and she learned rapidly to be effective, skilled—and brave. In the mornings she insisted on opening the windows to try to counteract the foul smells of the place where the odours from wounds, kitchens, washrooms and stables grew more and more overpowering through the day. 'A more perfect pestilence box than this house I never saw.' She describes the hospital as being '—cold, damp and dirty . . . no competent head male or female to right matters, and a jumble of good, bad and indifferent nurses, surgeons and

attendants to complicate chaos still more.' Even the
December climate of Washington, which rendered the place
draughty and chilly, contributed to the discomfort, if not
the danger, of the surroundings to her patients and herself.
But she records, though often homesick, heartsick and
worn out, 'I like it'.

Like it she did indeed, for she was doing work that
brought heartening results. Although, in the midst of the
deplorable surgical and hospital procedure of that time, she
lost many patients, she saw many go forward to recovery
or partial recovery, often rescued by her good care alone.
She had what few other nurses had, a vital interest in her
patients as individuals, an instinct for understanding them
and attending to their personal problems as well as their
physical needs. She wrote letters to mothers, wives and
sweethearts for them. She received their confidences when,
in the loneliness of desperate illness, they had no one else
to talk to. She listened to their terrible doubts as to whether
the young women they expected to marry would still be
willing to take them when they came home maimed and
crippled. And over and over she had to write to parents
something of their son's last days and that he would not
come home to them.

She was in a world so unlike anything she had known
before that it seemed scarcely less unreal than that of those
over-romantic tales by which she had been supporting her
cherished family. She wanted those at home to see it all
just as it was and, in the dark watches of night duty, as she
sat by some patient's bed, she would write to them letters
which she tried to make as direct and graphic as she could.
There was no piling-up of the horrors of war: they need

bear no more than the exact truth. All the details were before her; there was no need for imagination now.

She was completely unused to this kind of life, to the foul air, the bad food, the constant emotional strain of keeping up spirits, her own and those of others, in this desert of pain and death. In the end the task proved to be beyond her. She began to feel ill; she had a cold so severe that she would seek some quiet spot in a closet or on a back stair where she would cough until her whole anatomy seemed to be coming apart. She was at length unable to keep on her feet and was ordered by the doctor to remain in her room.

Diagnosis revealed that she had typhoid fever, complicated by accompanying pneumonia. The matron of the hospital, Mrs Ropes, was similarly ill with the same complaint. Days passed and Louisa, scarcely even knowing where she was, still insisted that she must be up and about her work. Then, suddenly, there was someone at the door, a familiar step, a familiar voice. Bronson Alcott spoke. 'I have come to take you home.'

At first, with the unreasoning obstinacy of the desperately ill, she refused to go. There was a little waiting. Mrs Ropes died. Almost her last order had been the message sent to Louisa's father to come to fetch his daughter home. Louisa, beginning to feel alarmingly worse, consented at last. It took courage for both of them to set out on such a journey. Her warm friends in the hospital, for she understandingly had a great many, wrapped her in shawls, gathered a basket of small comforts, got her to the train. Bronson managed to get her to Boston where she spent a night with relatives and had a sudden upsurge of terrible illness. He succeeded in bringing her home at last. Afterwards she could only remember dimly seeing May's shocked face at the railroad station and her mother's bewildered one at the house. Then she descended into a world where she recognized no one and whirled through sights and sounds such as her wildest flights of fantastic imagination had never conceived. Three weeks later she came to herself, almost unrecognizable when she looked at herself in a mirror, her long hair cropped, her face a pale ghost of the once vigorous Louisa.

Very slowly she came back to her ordinary life, first doing a little work about the house. It was when she was really convalescent that her father came in with the wonderful news that Anna had a son and that he was now a grandparent. For Louisa it was an inspiring delight that sped her on her way to recovery. When she finally was able to go to Boston where the Pratts were then living she saw 'our baby' and thought him ugly but promising. She got out her novel *Moods* and began to work on it once more. Meanwhile, however, her literary career had been advancing without her. The editor of the newspaper, the *Commonwealth*, had happened to see some of her letters home and was so impressed with their vividness and graphic simplicity that he asked permission to publish them. A number appeared in his paper and were read avidly. So many people who had relatives at the front were anxious to know how their boys would fare if they were wounded and, though Louisa had spared no details of the confusion and inefficiency at the hospital, the letters still managed to tell much of what they wanted to know.

After she got better the publishing firm of Redpath asked

to make a book out of the letters under the title, *Hospital Sketches*. As other editions were asked for, she added more accounts, so that not all the contents were strictly reprints of the letters. Another company, Roberts Brothers, also asked for the *Sketches* but Louisa chose Redpath.

A few years earlier, Louisa's father had shown some of her earlier fanciful stories to an editor who was a personal friend. The friend had examined them and had sent the message, 'Tell Louisa to stick to her teaching; she will never be a writer.' On hearing this encouraging dictum Louisa responded indignantly to her father, that she *would* become a writer and that she would see her stories published in his friend's magazine. It was thus that the editor of the *Atlantic* earned the privilege of publishing the best short story that Louisa every wrote, 'My Contraband'; in the *Atlantic* it had the title 'The Brothers'. It was one of the best pieces of writing to come out of the Civil War, and depicts the confrontation of the coloured orderly at the hospital with the wounded white officer, both sons of the same father. The story was written for the later edition of *Hospital Sketches*. It shows, as nothing else does, the profound change which was coming over Louisa's writing after this experience of the hospital and her illness and the full encounter with the tragedies of life.

There was no return to the melodramatic tales which had, earlier, been her daily bread. She busied herself with a complete revision of *Moods*, for this first novel was for long her favourite child. After much work on it she carried it to Mr Loring. *Hospital Sketches* were making the name of Louisa Alcott so well known that he undertook to publish

53

the novel. It had good reviews at first, but fell off in popularity very quickly. People evidently wanted something
else when they took up a book by Louisa. She had put so
much effort and so much hope into *Moods* that she might
have been very unhappy over this development, had not
a new change of circumstances come to her rescue.

No person as enterprising and as adventurous as Louisa
could fail to have a craving for travel. She had long desired
to go abroad; her very sense of the romance of far-off
things made the idea alluring. But for such a very long
time it had been utterly beyond her means. Now, after the
success of *Hospital Sketches*, the encouraging offers from
various publishers for more of her work made her begin
to feel cautiously prosperous. After the lengthy stagnation
of her illness and the return of energy, she was feeling
restless and more than ready for something new.

At this juncture, a friend of the family asked her whether
she would consider going abroad with his invalid daughter
who could not make the journey alone. Travel abroad
was considered, at that time, to be a panacea for all ills.
Knowing how good a nurse Louisa was, he felt that this
would be a thoroughly practical arrangement. His daughter
did not really need much nursing, yet she wanted companionship. Knowing also what good company Louisa was,
he was certain that this would be a fortunate choice for
both of them. Would Louisa go?

She hesitated over a decision. It might be that she would
never be able to go abroad in any other way. It seemed
foolish to relinquish such an opportunity, even though
certain aspects of the plan looked faintly doubtful. But so
great was her desire, and so earnest was the encouragement

she received from all sides, she finally consented. She
sailed on the *China* in July 1865, with a heart and a mind
wide open to receive new experience and new knowledge.

v. Thomas Niles

Atlantic crossings were long in those days, but there has been no change in the thrill of excitement when the shores of Europe are seen for the first time, rising out of an ocean which has seemed heretofore to be illimitable. Then, if the voyage is to England, there comes the passing of the green shores of Ireland, the coming in at dingy docks, the first walk through the streets with sea legs trying to adjust to a pavement that does not heave up and down underfoot. There is the first meal on land, the sign 'Fish and chips' and the American traveller knows that he is at last abroad.

Louisa brought to this journey a fund of eager and completely unsophisticated enthusiasm, a mature and appreciative mind, and a solid block of reading which made her ready to get the most out of every moment of new impressions. She was a devoted follower of Charles Dickens and had carried volumes of his work to the Georgetown Hospital where she had read aloud to her patients with great and comforting effect. Now she saw Dickens's characters everywhere, in the names on the signs, in the people moving past in so much less of a hurry than they did at home, in the Old Curiosity Shop, still extant and untouched.

They crossed the Channel from Dover, proceeded through Belgium and embarked on a journey by boat up the Rhine. Here Louisa's exuberant fancy met the reality of romance as it had once been lived by real people. They went by picturesque towns that crowded down steep slopes to the water side; they saw the churches and the castles crowning the hilltops behind . . . She looked back now, with clear-seeing eyes, to the time when she had written about dukes and duchesses, about battlements and dungeons. Who was she to have tried to write of them when she knew nothing at all of what they were like? She was done with that phase of her writing life, done for ever. She was learning to see in perspective not only the far past, but also, in comparison, the vigorous and exciting present.

They stopped finally at Schwalbach, where her companion was to take the cure. Here they prepared for a considerable stay. It was here that she set down a revealing item in her Journal: 'Still at Schwalbach, A. doing her best to get well and I doing mine to help her. Rather dull days, bathing, walking and quiddling about.' She had seen much that she had put away in her mind to think of and assimilate later; she found much to interest her now. But she was restless and had begun to be bored. She realized that all along the way she had wanted to see and do, while her friend was disinclined for too much effort and liked to stay quietly in one spot where she could be comfortable. At every stopping place Louisa had to deny herself things that she would have liked to see but had to pass by because she felt that she should not leave her charge for any length of time.

Now at Vevay the friend, to whom she always refers as A., settled placidly to enjoy peace and rest while Louisa seethed with inner impatience. Here were all the quaint small towns with all their richness of a past age; here were also the stupendous beauties of the snow-covered Alps.

So much to go unvisited because A. was unwilling to make sufficient exertion. The journey so far had been glorious at times, but often mingled with disappointment. Was she to consider it a failure? It was at this point that the future Laurie entered the picture.

He arrived at the Pension Victoria where the two travellers were staying; a pale, thin Polish boy not yet twenty years old, a young revolutionary who had been imprisoned and then sent into exile. He was under the threat of tuberculosis on account of his months of imprisonment. As he was introduced round the dinner table, Louisa, as was like her, noticed how weary-looking he was from his long journey in the diligence. She observed, after they sat down, that he was shivering in a draughty place at the table, too far removed from the big porcelain stove. She saw to it that his seat was exchanged with hers which she found uncomfortably hot. He came later to thank her and from that moment the two were friends.

The acquaintance grew and flourished with great rapidity, as it does when two people realize that their time together is short. She came to understand him fully: his patriotic ideals, his passion for music and for his poor country of Poland, lying prostrate under Russian dominance. She was deeply troubled by the evidences of his ill health. In his turn he offered her frank and unstinted devotion. Accustomed to the sterner manner of her New England compatriots, Louisa found this intense and open adoration both astonishing and delightful. It was a true and sincere-hearted friendship that could hardly be matched anywhere, and it was immensely good for her. She had faced overwhelming odds so many times that she could never be really sure of herself. But here was an unquestioning and undemanding belief in her that made for much-needed reassurance.

Many things had come along to change her in the last two years: her sharp and sudden acquaintance with reality in those weeks in the hospital, her long illness with its period of convalescence and leisure for reflection, her unexpected literary success with the publication of *Hospital Sketches*. And here, with an exhilarating change of scene, was this full-hearted admiration from someone close to her.

It was this final touch that seemed to open the door to a new creative ability and her awareness of it.

There is no doubt that the two friends, in their long walks and talks together, told each other much of themselves, their ideals, their feelings towards life and its possibilities. What Ladislas Wisniewski got from the relationship we do not know, but what Louisa achieved was a full and clear perspective of her own on matters around her, especially on her people at home of whom she thought incessantly. It was a satisfaction to know that her father was happily settling into his chosen work of passing on his cherished philosophical opinions by means of his Conversations. They were at last being recognized and even becoming financially profitable. But it could not be denied that her mother was growing older and more feeble; yet Anna was fully content in her little home with a loving husband for whom Louisa felt greater and greater respect and regard, and her two little sons. Her sister May was growing up a talented and dedicated artist, full of energy and spirit, very like Louisa's own. Her sister determined that there must be some way open for this younger member of her family to fulfil her ambitions, so like Louisa's. Art could be studied and furthered; writing Louisa had been obliged to learn for herself, by trial and error. Her family responsibilities had grown fewer with Elizabeth's death and Anna's marriage, but here was a great opportunity showing itself for insuring a happy future for May. Louisa had been content to sacrifice everything to accomplish the welfare and security of her beloved family: May wished above all things to be great and famous. By earlier arrangement Louisa and her friend moved on to spend the winter in Nice. She and Laurie said goodbye.

In Italy they were joined by other friends of A.'s. After a little interval Louisa determined that her obligations had been fulfilled. A. would no longer be alone if Louisa went home. Agreement was quickly reached. Louisa, at brief notice, packed her effects and went on her way 'feeling as happy as a freed bird', she said. She was to visit Paris, and London again, and then—home.

In Paris she was to see Ladislas once more; in fact he was at the station to meet her, having inquired steadily at the pension where he had heard that she was to stay. He arranged that she saw the sights of Paris properly, and guided her through a gay and glittering city for two dizzy weeks. The Emperor of France, Napoleon III, and his beautiful Empress, were carrying out to the full their idea that a brilliant and spectacular reign would insure the stability of the rather uncertain throne which the great Napoleon had left behind. But after this brief stay Louisa said goodbye again to Ladislas. It was hard, for he cried out desperately, 'I shall never see you again.' It was, nevertheless, no misfortune that such a perfect friendship should end before anything came to spoil it and the memory of it.

Louisa already had friends in London, while letters from publishers in America opened further doors to her. She visited country houses where she was warmly entertained. But nothing stayed the plan of her progress, for above all things she was going home. Her mother was at the door of Orchard House to receive her, weeping with happiness and relief. Louisa had been gone almost exactly a year.

After the excitement of arrival had settled down and the gifts had been distributed, Louisa set herself to take stock of the family situation. It was not cheering. She could see, after long absence, how much her mother had aged. She was less than a year older than her husband but while Bronson was ruddy, serene and able as ever, Abba was not. She had said in a letter to Bronson before she married him, 'I do not expect to gather flowers all my life'. Her days had indeed been spent doing very far from that, but she had never complained or looked back since the day she was married. Now it was very clear that she had far less strength than in her earlier vigorous days, a thing which young persons are never prepared to see in their elders. Louisa's often expressed desire to give her mother 'a sunny room where she could rest and be free from worry' was still far from being fulfilled.

A very few questions revealed the fact that, to keep the family afloat while their main breadwinner was away, it had been necessary to borrow money. It was the repayment of this loan that Louisa set herself as her first task.

Her book *Moods* had added nothing to her reputation, but her stories were still in popular demand. She had regular assignments for so many stories a month, longer or shorter, at better rates. She worked so busily that she had practically no time for rest. She was more or less restored to health and had very definitely regained her good spirits and she was assailed from all sides with requests for work. In September 1867, little more than a year after her return from Europe, she received two very definite propositions. She was asked to be editor of a magazine, *Merry's Museum*. This entailed reading manuscripts and writing a story a month with as many editorials. She was to receive $500 a year. She said she would try it. At the same time she was asked by the chief editor of the publishing firm of Roberts Brothers to 'write a story for girls'. This request she put aside since she had no interest in it.

On the strength of the editorship she arranged to take a room in Boston, a 'sky parlour' where she could work in quiet, since, as she now admitted, she could never keep well in Concord. She has said of her siege with typhoid during the war that she had never been ill before it and was never well after it, but she did not let this fact interfere with her capacity for hard work. In *An Old-Fashioned Girl* she describes her entry into Boston, riding on a farmer's cart with all her wordly possessions about her and a squash pie in her hand presented at the last minute by an admiring friend. Here she became so absorbed in the immediate business of fulfilling her engagements that the request of Roberts Brothers was entirely forgotten. It was not until May 1868 that the same person, Thomas Niles, made it again. He still wanted 'a book for girls'.

He was a most astute editor. He had read and approved *Hospital Sketches* and saw deeper into their qualities than any reader or other editor had done. Here was a young writer of vigour and promise, capable, moreover, of entering a field which, he was quite certain, was a truly important one. Louisa still hesitated, even though she had not taken very kindly to editorial work and had not yet been paid. She insisted that she did not understand girls and that boys interested her more. She sent her father to Mr Niles to ask him if he did not want a fairy book. He did not.

Louisa seems by this time to have succeeded in paying off the debt which her mother had been obliged to incur. But other needs were pressing. She told Roberts Brothers reluctantly that she would try and with many doubts she set herself to work. For a long time she had had at the back of her mind a plan to write her father's story, of his boyhood on a farm, of the Temple School, of Fruitlands and what had come after. Her plan was to call it *The Cost of an Idea*. As the thought grew it seemed to her to be more like a household chronicle and she thought of naming it *The Pathetic Family*. This title was quickly dropped since of all things that the Alcotts might be, they certainly never thought of themselves as pathetic. But Elizabeth's illness had intervened and the idea was not developed.

It recurred to her now and must have been, in fact, much nearer to the surface of her mind than she realized, so easily and quickly did it shape itself the moment she began to write. She set down the first scene; the four March girls talking by the fire on Christmas Eve.

One sees at once her mastery of character. In those first paragraphs, every speech, as in turn the girls voice their plans for Christmas, is completely in character and never varies from that image throughout the whole of the book. Each always speaks exactly as herself, each is strictly the same individual as first presented in that opening scene.

Having once got under way, the story proceeded with remarkable rapidity. Louisa was at home in Concord when she began to write in May and by June had sent Thomas Niles the first twelve chapters. On first inspection he pronounced them dull, as did also the doubting Louisa. But she had come to share his view that 'lively, simple books are very much needed for girls' and so went steadily on. In less than another month she had finished and confided to her Journal, 'Very tired, head full of pain from overwork and heart heavy about Marmee who is growing feeble'.

Once more Thomas Niles showed his astuteness as an editor. He was unmarried, but he belonged to a very large family and had a host of nieces and nephews in whom he took the greatest interest. He presented the manuscript to one of his nieces and asked her opinion on it. She and a group of friends exclaimed over their utter absorption in it, pronounced their verdict as 'splendid' and recommended it without reservation.

Thomas Niles banished his own doubts. He made Louisa an outright offer for the copyright, but being the fairest of men, he advised her to take royalties instead. He had formally accepted the manuscript by July 15th, 1868, and by a distinct feat, since he wanted it for the Christmas sales, he got it out by October. He asked Louisa for a title. It was really Bronson who supplied it. He had long since been accustomed to speak of his daughters as his Little Women. It was thus that the remarkable book was born.

Louisa read the proofs in August, since she was at home,

supposedly for some rest, which ended as it always did in vigorous toil at housework. Her mother was not well, Anna was absorbed in her babies, May busy with an increasing number of her drawing classes. 'We don't like the kitchen department,' Louisa said of herself and May. 'Our tastes and gifts lie in other directions so it is hard to make the various Pegasuses pull the plan steadily.'

As for *Little Women*, the book's success has only been matched by its longevity. All of a sudden everyone was reading it, exclaiming over it, recommending it to everyone else, cherishing Jo in their hearts, twittering over Meg's romance, grieving over Elizabeth's illness. Very few family copies of the book are not marked by the tears shed over those brief, moving passages. By October, soon after the book came out, Louisa returned to Boston, took another sky-parlour room and settled to work again. It had become plain that a sequel was being earnestly demanded. Young readers declared they must know whom the March girls married. Louisa began on November 1st and set out to write a chapter a day. She did exactly that and was finished by New Year's Day. 'I *won't* marry Jo to Laurie to please anyone,' she declared firmly, and added, 'I am so full of my work that I can't stop to eat or sleep, or for anything but a daily run.' She had written both volumes in eight months. Now in its completion it was a greater success than ever.

What was it that she had put into *Little Women* that enlisted such a delighted reception by everyone who read it, such enthusiastic praise everywhere? Perhaps, for the first time, Louisa Alcott offered a completely true chronicle of an American family exactly as it was. As weeks went on and the thousands of readers rose to tens of thousands it became evident that here under the slight veil of fiction was not merely a story of a family, but the American Family Story as an institution of its own, to take its firm place in the body of children's literature.

VI. Plumfield

The thinking world has only recently taken note of the fact
that literature for children is an entity in itself, with its
own qualities, its own history, its own development. It has
remained free, as adult literature has not, from unreasoned
changes in pattern and content, and from demands to
satisfy tastes for the incomprehensible in style and the
erotic in mood. Yet we can say that when Louisa Alcott
wrote a book which was natural, honest and true to ordinary
life, and which, further, was of such popularity that it
permeated practically the whole of the reading public of
that day, she was of great influence in determining the
direction in which juvenile literature was to go. It was,
moreover, not one book, but the beginning of a whole
series, unlike in characters and content, but always con-
sistent in their salient qualities, which carried on the new
tradition. As a result of her success, other writers followed
her illuminating example for which we may be happily
thankful.

'There is no sensationalism in it,' she said of *Little
Women* when she finished it. She had made a great effort,
also, to keep out both preaching and sentimentalism. But
it must be remembered that she wrote in a different age
from ours, one with its own pronounced customs and
standards. Her characters are so lifelike that young people
tend to think of them as of their own time, so that they
are startled when Meg buys twenty-five yards of silk for

a dress and when Mr March declares that his overcoat was stolen so that he was obliged to buy a shawl. Tom Shaw, in *An Old-Fashioned Girl*, is shocked when he finds that his fiancée 'paints', meaning that she uses cosmetics. Manners of the day allowed far greater freedom of discussion of inward feelings than is approved now, but matched present-day reticence by a careful taboo on the mention of legs, which are now so thoroughly and happily in the public eye. All humanity knows that sentiment is one of the well-springs of true living. Critics of today find sentimentality in Louisa's writing, but it is far less in extent and kind than in other writers of her time and is certainly not the artificial straining after emotion which is its true definition. Nor did she truly preach. She shared some experiences of living with young readers, especially her own experience in learning to control an explosive temper, just as her mother had done battle with hers. Marmee's analysis of temper is worth remembering. She is speaking of John Brooke, Meg's very new husband. 'He has a temper—not like ours—one flash and then it is all over—but the white still anger that is seldom stirred but once kindled is hard to quench.' Much of what is described as preaching is merely Marmee's sharing with her children of the knowledge of living that life has brought her. Often Louisa does no more than voice what parents of today would like to tell their children but do not attempt for they think the children would not listen. They are glad indeed to have Louisa say it for them.

It has been said by some that *Little Women* has virtually no plot, and yet the story does most remarkably hang together. The plot is in the character development of young people learning to make the most of all that is in them, to prepare for the responsibilities and problems which will come upon them later. Louisa has said that the figure of Mr March is not that of her father, but of her beloved uncle Samuel May. She never used Bronson Alcott as a model for any of her characters. It is evident that he was, to her, just as much an enigma as he is to posterity. She would have had to look for a way of doing justice to a parent who was singularly lacking in a sense of responsibility towards his family, a fact which redoubled her own. Yet her definition of a philosopher as a man in a balloon with all his family tugging at the ropes to hold him down to earth is a metaphor of pure love.

Both Bronson and Anna insisted that the model for Laurie was a certain Llewellyn Willis, a young man who had boarded with the Alcotts at different times, first when they were at Still River. But Louisa has said, herself, that it was the Polish boy at Vevay who stood for the portrait of Laurie. He, next to Jo, is the most successful character in the book, for Louisa has captured something of that boy's real charm, his volatile spirit, and his dark good looks.

When the second part of *Little Women* (known to many as *Good Wives*) was ready for publication, Louisa was well-nigh worn out, for she had worked under very great pressure. With the advent of prosperity the whole picture of her life changed suddenly. Everyone was praising her, desiring to meet her, the famous Miss Alcott, the talk of the town. She soon learned that fame can be a great complication to life and she wished above all things to avoid it. Prosperity had made it possible for her and her family to live in greater comfort and without anxieties, but it had not brought her one much-needed thing, the opportunity to rest. Roberts Brothers, the publishers of *Little Women*, were anxious to have her go forward at once and make the most of her public's enthusiasm while it was at its full height.

Mr and Mrs Alcott were spending that winter of 1869 with Anna, who was living in Boston with her little family. May joined Louisa to have her drawing classes in Louisa's apartment. The house in Concord was closed, and Louisa and May went to shut it up. Louisa had never liked it and said that she rejoiced as she turned the key for the last time. The place was too closely associated with the saddest years of her life, the time of Elizabeth's death and of Anna's departure from the family. It was haunted, too, by the memory of those weeks of delirium and suffering. She and May briefly tried a sojourn at the Hotel Bellevue on Beacon Hill, but they found it so unhomelike that they presently took rooms on Pinckney Street, where Louisa began *An Old-Fashioned Girl*.

Besides being so weary, Louisa fell ill with laryngitis, but worked steadily on. 'I wrote it with left hand in a sling,' she says of the book, 'one foot up, head aching and no voice.' Since the book had some amusing passages people seemed to think that she had rollicked through it and asked if she had not enjoyed doing it. She enjoyed having made such a deceptive impression. Ever since the typhoid experience she had been greatly troubled by neuralgia and neuritis, with almost constant pain. 'But', as she said, 'I would rather sit and scribble than lie and groan.'

The new book was not a long one and was published in

March 1870. By this time it was evident that Louisa must have some definite respite. A friend was going abroad, who offered to pay May's expenses to travel with her, if Louisa would consent to go too. It proved to be a most delightful plan. They sailed in April directly to Brest.

In the book which she left behind her to win new success, she had once more made use of her own experiences. At the time when she had set out to make her own way and to support herself, such an attempt was looked upon by society as something not only peculiar but not quite proper. It was better, so her class of society thought, to spend one's life as a dependent in some home of more fortunate relatives, than to look for security and independence of one's own. Louisa had never voiced abroad that determination 'to take Fate by the throat and shake a living out of her'. If she had done so it would have been considered utterly shocking.

People who could remember that time, have said that *An Old-Fashioned Girl* is a remarkably true picture of Boston society of that day, with its traditions, its conventions, its taboos of various kinds, few of them dictated by reason, its attitude of defence against strangers, its warm-hearted friendships in the narrow circle wherein they seemed justified. Yet Louisa, wherever she went, seemed always to find out the kindly, usually elderly woman, often poor but always with some young protégé at hand to whom she would give what she could and for whom she could interest others into accomplishing even more.

The new story was also a family chronicle, both of the Shaws, whom Polly visited in the city at the opening of the book, and of Polly Milton's own family, in the persons of Polly and her slightly younger brother and their firm loyalty to each other. It is easy for a reader, in the interest of finding just how things are going to turn out, to pass over the character drawing of Fanny Shaw, who is so faithful to her friend Polly from the country, even though her own associates have no better taste than to look down upon the gay and plucky little girl who is a wage-earner. Fanny always invites Polly to the meetings of the 'sewing circle' whose gatherings are far more social occasions than for any output of work. Polly has only one best gown and she hears one guest whisper to the others about 'that inevitable dress'.

There is neither exaggeration nor bitterness in this account of what a girl struggling for her self-support goes through. Polly here is not Louisa in person as Jo March was; she is smaller, more cheerfully tolerant, but just as full of indomitable spirit. In return for Fanny's so stoutly standing by her, she introduces that rather bored and restless girl to a group of her own friends all of whom are doing constructive and able work. In the studio where one of them is carrying on her pursuit of sculpture, Fanny meets the room-mate who supports herself by cutting wood blocks, and various friends, each with her own occupation. If there is any self-portrait here it is Kate, 'who has written a successful book by accident, and happened to be the fashion just then', but who looks, as Louisa describes her, 'tired and too-early old'.

The success of *An Old-Fashioned Girl* proved clearly that Louisa had not written a good book 'by accident' and that she was thoroughly and reasonably launched as a widely-beloved writer for girls—and their parents. She had managed to pay not only the new debt incurred while she was away, but all the old ones, even the doctor's bill for the care of Elizabeth in her last months, although that account was eight years old. And now a fresh thought occurred to her. She could, with a clear conscience, spend some money on herself! It was with a light heart and a free mind that she set out on her journey.

There was a happy similarity of tastes and desires among the three travellers, who moved or tarried according to the immediate impulse and who went here or there as they felt inclined. Louisa could not do as much sight-seeing as the others but she never let them feel hampered in their plans on that account. Although years later Louisa, weary of being pursued by publicity, destroyed all the letters which her mother had so carefully preserved over the years, her father in this case made copies of her letters home and they have been preserved for us. The account of their journeyings is full of laughter, gay adventure and whole-hearted enjoyment, all this in spite of the fact that the neuralgia and neuritis which had troubled her so long were inexorably still with her. She relates that May sketched and painted to her heart's content, A.B. shopped 'and I dawdled after them.'

They came presently to Rome, where they expected to make a lengthy stay, but here the happy journey was interrupted by dismaying news from home. John Pratt, Anna's husband, died suddenly, leaving his wife and two small children quite unprovided for. What did this mean to Louisa? It meant, just as every family crisis did, the assuming of new responsibility and the setting at once to hard work again. It was thus that *Little Men* came into being, to ensure Anna's welfare and that of the little boys. Louisa completed it in London, mailed it to her publishers and very soon after, followed it home. Her father and Thomas Niles met her as the ship docked. They had pinned up in the carriage a large red placard which announced that 50,000 copies of *Little Men* had been sold before publication. It had appeared first in London, and now came out in the United States the day that Louisa landed in June 1871.

Louisa had said more than once that she understood boys rather better than girls. Thus she was in her glory when she began the account of that Plumfield School for which plans were in the making at the close of *Little Women*. The establishment of that fictitious school was really a monument to her father's educational theories, for here are embodied the ideas for which his memory deserves so much credit and for which he suffered so much obloquy as he tried to carry them out. When transmitted through the practical mind of his daughter Louisa they are bequeathed to our age as a system of knowing children as individuals, as recognizing their spiritual capacity and their spiritual needs as well as their bodily and intellectual ones. They were for making the acquisition of learning a rewarding experience of aroused and satisfied curiosity, instead of an arbitrary infliction of undigested facts. *Little Men* is still a family story. Because a family's needs were always her incentive and inspiration, it came to be the direct subject which brought out the best of her writing.

All the characters whom we came to know in *Little Women* take their own parts in connection with the school,

Laurie as consultant and patron, Mr and Mrs March ready
to give advice at need, with Meg and Amy as mothers of
the younger children who have their own part in the school
life. We meet Jo again, the same energetic and entertaining
person. This imaginary projection of herself as married,
with two sons, and as the able centre of a lively and complicated educational institution, is indeed convincing enough,
even though we know that this Jo is pure fiction.

The school is small, with only twelve boys, but we see
very clearly Louisa's talent in her rapid summary of the
personalities of each one as seen through the eyes of some-
body who thoroughly understands them. There is Nat, the
boy rescued from the depths of poverty-stricken surroundings which have taught him by harsh necessity to fall into
the habit of lying, who musters sufficient strength of
character to get over it. There is Dan, the boy much further
gone into the corrupting state of mind and spirit that
loneliness and sheer destitution can produce. The others
are children of better-off households, each with his own
problems, each meeting life in his own way. We are not
likely soon to forget Tommy Bangs, absurd and endearing,
always in trouble of his own making, and always extricating
himself with unfailing talent. Dan, whose fierce wild spirit
is one of Louisa's most interesting personalities, is not to
be tamed even by Plumfield and has to be sent away as a
harmful influence, but he makes a good friend in the
naturalist, Mr Hyde, who finds him a kindred spirit and
through his interest in animals and all living things, manages to lead him to another attitude of life. The naturalist
is very plainly Henry David Thoreau. One watches with
respect how skilfully Louisa carries them all forward, such

a number of characters none of whom ever lose their individuality.

As we have seen, Louisa was always interested in private theatricals, so that very few of her books fail to recount some dramatic presentation, each of its own original kind. One of the best of these occasions occurs in *Little Men* in the Thanksgiving Revels. A gigantic pumpkin has been produced in the Plumfield garden, so large that Mrs Jo bases the action of the evening upon it. There are other plays but the final one is 'Cinderella' with Amy's very small daughter as heroine. She is discovered sitting dolefully beside the fire; a fairy godmother appears and, at the wave of her wand, the ragged pinafore disappears and little Elizabeth is now seen dressed as a court lady, in flowered silk with a long satin train. The huge pumpkin, now on wheels, comes lumbering in, and Cinderella actually gets into it, and is rolled away, her small feet in their silverpaper slippers sticking out in front and her satin train protruding from the back. The book ends with the gay revels still in progress, Jo and Laurie looking on, quietly discussing their charges and their probable futures. These two are still one in that unquestioning friendship which is the finest of Louisa's creations.

The expedition abroad had done much, for the moment, for Louisa's health. But the results were only temporary and, after going busily to work immediately after her return, the good effects wore off within a month. It was not poverty which pursued her but publishers and their desire to make the most of what her intense popularity would afford. She returned to work on the novel which she called *Success* although it was published under the title of *Work*.

It was not the memorable book her others had been, for she was here outside her real field. It was published in 1873, shortly after a little book called *Shawl-Straps*, this last being more or less an account of her journey abroad. She had been obliged to call May home, but, as she learned to work a little less vehemently and her health improved somewhat, she sent May abroad again for further study in England while she herself sat down to the writing of *Eight Cousins*, and the sequel which was to follow it. She was glad indeed to be able to do this for her ambitious sister, and it was with a happy heart that she saw May off in September 1876. But she was never to see her again.

VII. Plumfield Revisited

Already knowing what the future demand would be, Louisa promised even in the preface of *Eight Cousins* that there would be a sequel. She allowed herself plenty of boys among the characters in the book. She had plenty of models to study, for Boston was positively alive with cousins of the May family, so many that we have no way of knowing which Sewell, Warren or May stood for in the resulting story. The Campbells who make up the family were more than simply young relatives: since their descent was Scottish they had organized themselves into a clan. Seven boys and one girl make up the company, with an assortment of aunts, uncles and parents in appropriate numbers.

The story has the background, not of Boston's social traditions and conventions but of its fine, materially prosperous days when fortunes were being made in the East India trade and comfortable wealth was widespread. Rose, the heroine, is heir to large possessions in her own right; she visits the ship of one of her wealthy uncles; she is given Oriental gifts by him and her guardian, Uncle Alec. Louisa slips in an extra boy in the person of the young Chinaman, Fun See, who has come to America to be educated. The story does not take any very great notice of him, but in the sequel he marries a Boston girl of established family, a slightly incongruous note which Louisa does not often allow herself.

The study is again that of the effect of character on

character, and the development of various persons as they all grow up together. Louisa does not often take on so large a cast of characters, but her hand does not slip other than with the Chinese marriage. She does full duty by all of them. On the one hand is Rose, an orphan in the care of her aunts until her uncle, Dr Alec Campbell, comes home from India to take charge of her and her affairs. Her able and bustling Aunt Plenty, with various consulting aunts hovering in the background, all agree that Rose is delicate and must be taken out of the school where her father had placed her before he died, and must be very tenderly cared for. While her gentle Aunt Peace, who lives with Aunt Plenty, slightly demurs from this idea, she makes no definite stand. It is left to Uncle Alec and the seven boy cousins to make short work of any such intentions.

We see Rose at the opening of the book in a shy flutter, preparing to receive the first call from the troop of seven, whom she takes at first to be a circus, driving a gay dog-cart or mounted on ponies. Archie as the acknowledged head of the clan introduces each, with Rose more and more confused as she tries to remember names and faces. Besides Archie there is the good-looking and dashing Charley, there is the bookworm Mac, and the very down-to-earth and dandified Steve—beyond that she loses count. But the boys are deeply impressed by their pretty cousin and are sorry for her.

We do not have, in this book, any recognizable self-portrait of Louisa, but Uncle Alec, who appears on the scene the next day, is the able spokesman for many of her ideas of a young person's rights and needs. The development of the story lies in the strengthening and enlarging of

Rose's self-confidence and her knowledge of the world about her. Treatment at the boys' hands in this direction is kindly but somewhat rough for they do not hesitate to tease her and to treat her as one of themselves. A great test comes one day when, on going into her doctor-guardian's special room, she sees a closet door swing open and knows, with a terrified gasp, that here is the skeleton which he keeps for medical study and that it is lifting a bony hand to beckon to her. But she hears a smothered giggle, looks more closely and sees a black thread through a hole behind the dreadful figure attached to the skeleton's bony hand. She pulls her trembling self together, whips out a pair of scissors from her pocket, cuts the thread and summons two dusty little boys to come out of hiding.

Uncle Alec sees to it that Rose's room in the somewhat overstuffed Victorian house is airy and full of sunshine; he breaks up a scene in which Rose has been dressed up by her aunts in a pinched and over-elaborate costume with high heels, an absurdly tilted little hat and a spotted veil tied over her small nose. Louisa manages to make the simple, comfortable and warm outfit provided by her uncle seem much more attractive. The aunts are routed, one of them guiltily concealing the small corset which she had not dared to display before her stern brother.

Rose shows her spirit by making friends with Phoebe, the girl from the poorhouse who works in the kitchen. Possessed of a beautiful voice but with no opportunity for its training, Phoebe is a strong and interesting character. Rose resists with spirit the aunts' objections to her making such a friend, whom she insists on 'adopting'.

There arrived in 1876, a year after *Eight Cousins* was

published, the promised sequel *Rose in Bloom*. In it there is much buzzing among the aunts as to which of the cousins Rose should marry. Aunt Clara, the most worldly of the Campbell clan, says Rose's fortune must 'be kept in the family'. In the end Rose makes her own and somewhat unexpected choice. Through both books a reader is so much interested in the separate people that it is easy to overlook the rare skill with which Louisa manages her large group of characters and holds them all together.

No matter how weary and ailing she might be, Louisa never lost the spirit of enterprising adventure. No matter how great her success in one quarter, she was always curious to try experiments in another. There came, after *Rose in Bloom*, a sudden and most unexpected opportunity of a sort that was after her own heart. Roberts Brothers had been issuing a succession of novels which they called *The No Name Series*. These were published anonymously, although it was known that they were usually by established writers. Each author was encouraged to disguise his style as far as he could and thus leave the public to guess the writer's name.

When Thomas Niles approached Louisa on the subject of contributing to the series she was delighted. She was always rapid in composition and, since this undertaking was one that she thoroughly enjoyed, she made no delay. *A Modern Mephistopheles* was published in April 1877. She had looked forward to the moment of its appearance and said in a letter to Thomas Niles, 'Now the fun will begin.'

Actually, she could not very well disguise her style, which was as direct and straightforward as Louisa herself. But she could vary her subject matter and this she did by returning, thus briefly, to the old ultra-romantic phase, reminiscent of Bettine von Arnim and *The Mysteries of Udolpho*. It is difficult to do justice to a piece of work which was so much short of Louisa's excellence but it is true that the story, as Loring had once said, 'had plenty of plot' and that it is absorbing as one reads it, all the time enjoying the thought of how much pleasure Louisa took in its ingenious composition.

She had chosen to offer a parallel to the Faust legend by which she had been so impressed in Goethe's version of it. The scene is supposedly contemporary, although there is no specific background. Because it is connected with legend it is clear enough that it is not intended to be taken as reality; certainly the characters are so incredible that nothing but intense over-writing can give them substance at all. The principal figure, Helwyze, is diabolically inspired to love power over others, and gains influence over Felix Canaris, a very minor poet who is wildly desirous of fame and public applause. He, of course, represents Faust. Marguerite is presented in the person of Gladys, full of quiet innocence, deeply in love with Canaris and married to him. Helwyze takes the pair into his household. Canaris suddenly begins to publish books of such power and success that he is intoxicated with delight over the fame which they bring him.

People who were trying to guess the identity of the book's author might have found a clue in the fact that here, as in so many of her stories, Louisa includes an amateur theatrical performance. She has described Helwyze's house as abounding in rich stuffs and curious jewellery brought home from distant lands, and she cannot resist making a dramatic spectacle out of them. She does not follow the Faust legend exactly, for she makes Helwyze fall in love with Gladys and her innocent goodness. He reveals to her the secret that he is the author of the books which he has allowed Canaris to publish as his own, and Gladys, already shattered by the unhappiness in that house, dies from the shock. The secret of the real book's authorship was not very well kept, but it was not until some years after Louisa's death that a new edition was brought out with her name attached. Printed with it is a short story 'A Whisper in the Dark', the one tale out of her past romantic phase which she had allowed to be republished.

There had been one more change of base for the Alcott household. Soon after the publication of *Rose in Bloom* with its attendant success, Louisa bought the Thoreau family house within the town of Concord. It was principally to make a home for Anna Pratt and her boys, but Louisa and her father and mother lived there also. At last Abba Alcott had that 'sunny room' where she could sit and be at rest from hard toil and pursuing anxieties. Louisa could feel that they were all free for good of Apple Slump, the name by which she had always referred to Orchard House. (The title is that of a very plain and not very appetizing New England dessert.) Henry David Thoreau had died at the age of forty-five, during that year of Louisa's working at the Georgetown Hospital. Next to Waldo Emerson he had been the Alcott family's closest friend. The house was smaller than Apple Slump, compact and comfortable. It was Bronson's base for his expeditions to the West to hold Conversations. Now he was hailed everywhere as 'the father of *Little Women*' which pleased him greatly. He called it 'riding in Louisa's chariot'. Louisa still spent much time in temporary quarters in Boston. She had settled down to like the Bellevue Hotel where they made her very comfortable and where *A Modern Mephistopheles* was written. She spent summers in Concord, but a note in her Journal recording 'ninety visitors in a month' tells something of why she sought quieter and less exposed quarters.

After her brief excursion into melodrama, Louisa settled to her next undertaking, that of writing a short serial for the *St Nicholas* which was making a name for itself as one of the best magazines for young people ever published. It is good to know what warm friendship grew up between her and Mary Mapes Dodge who, with a genius of her own sort matching Louisa's in quality, was introducing young people to a richness of literature they might otherwise never have known.

The serial was *Under the Lilacs*, a pleasant, pastoral little story with two small girls as joint heroines, a waif of a boy who has run away from a circus and, as an important member of the group of characters, a performing dog, a white poodle. Louisa made a careful visit to Van Amberg's circus in search of detailed information about what was to be expected of a talented highly-trained dog. The dog and his orphan master are taken in by a kind family and given a home. The action arises from the dog's being stolen, and after much effort, happily found again by one of the little girls. The story has a quieter tone than some of the others and is not so well remembered now. It has, however, that quality of homely happiness which was Louisa's special gift.

Much of the story was written in Concord, by her mother's bedside, for Abba Alcott, worn out by the hard work of a devoted life, was growing steadily more feeble. At one time Louisa herself was severely, even dangerously ill, but she gathered strength again and was able to nurse her mother to the end. Abba Alcott died in November 1877. May was still away and it seemed useless for her to come home, although Louisa was sorely lonely without her. Not many months later May was married in London to the Swiss merchant Ernest Nieriker.

In the next year, when Louisa was at work on *Jack and Jill*, she made hopeful plans to visit May in Muedon where she was expecting a child. In the end, however, the doctors persuaded Louisa not to undertake such a journey for, although she was better in health, the hazards of travel were obviously too much for her. News came in December 1879 that May had a daughter, to be named Louisa. Then there was an interval of silence. Three weeks later Waldo Emerson appeared at the door with a message. 'My child, I wish I could prepare you,' he began, 'but alas, alas!' May had died, passing from delirium into unconsciousness, but, foreseeing what might happen, she had directed that little Louisa be taken to her aunt in America. Ernest Nieriker had cabled the news to Emerson, knowing how devoted a friend he was. Louisa, gallant and stout of heart as always, took the tidings bravely, but they almost crushed her.

She knew that work would be her only solace while she waited for little Lulu to be brought to her, for the baby was not yet old enough to travel. Work did indeed come to her rescue, for *Jack and Jill* seems the gayest of all her books. One of the merits of Louisa's stories is the liveliness of the people in them, always doing briskly interesting things in a most energetic way. After reading one of her books one finds oneself suddenly feeling full of energy and good intentions. She had said, as she began the book, I 'have no plan yet but a boy, a girl and a sled with an upset to start with'. She goes steadily on from there, with the snowbanks of Concord, the laughing group of red-cheeked boys and girls and her hero and heroine preparing for a specially daring slide. Although the story has to do with injuries and a long period of recovery courageously endured, the general feeling is a most heartening one. No one knew more fully than Louisa that long illness necessarily brings a sort of dead despair and that it is only routed by gallantry of spirit. All the young friends stand faithfully by and what might be a dreary sickroom is presented as a crowded and hilarious centre for all the young life of the small town.

By the time little Louisa Nieriker was nearly a year old it was thought safe to bring her across the sea. Louisa had sent a reliable woman to fetch her, and now stood waiting on the Boston wharf full of pent-up emotion as the ship docked. Small Lulu had already made her own place among her fellow-passengers and was carried ashore in the arms of the captain himself. Louisa had made over the Concord house to Anna and had rented one in Boston in Louisburg Square. But it was not her house, it was Lulu's.

The days and weeks and years passed very tranquilly now, with Lulu growing up into a strong, healthy, always enterprising and often difficult child. She was greatly like

Louisa in temperament, and the two understood each other perfectly. She was indeed a comfort to Louisa's sore heart. In time Louisa began writing again although she resented the fact that she could no longer work fourteen hours a day. She bought a cottage at Nonquit for their weeks of holiday at the seashore, and rejoiced that it did not have 'the curse of a kitchen', there being a summer hotel close by. From time to time she would gather up her short stories, written for different ages of children, and publish them in collections, *Silver Pitchers*, *Spinning-Wheel Stories*, and others, those for the smallest children being *Lulu's Library*. The voices which had been raised years ago requesting a sequel to the still-loved *Little Men* were not silent, even yet, and Louisa began *Jo's Boys*.

There were many interruptions, illnesses of her own and other people's, distractions of various sorts. Seven years passed between the time she undertook it and its final finishing. She was known to have referred to it as 'those dreadful boys'. She toiled on, for it was continually being called for. Her health declined steadily; she was, as she said of Kate in *An Old-Fashioned Girl*, 'too-early old'. She was never to see real old age.

Her father had a paralytic stroke and was for long a helpless invalid. His later years had been brightened by the founding of the School of Philosophy in Concord, which had been his hopeful dream. He and Emerson held high positions in it. Orchard House was the scene of its first meetings, and a special building for its needs was erected in the grounds. The man who financed and founded the school was a Mr Harris of St Louis, who had once attended Bronson's Conversations and had never forgotten them. He bought Orchard House and lived there during the sessions of the school. Later it was bought by the Louisa May Alcott Memorial Association and has been made into a museum dedicated to the memory of the Alcott family.

In her Preface to *Jo's Boys* which was finally published in 1886, Louisa apologizes for the faults of the book, which were due to the multitude of interruptions that the writing of it had suffered. But the work needed no apology; no matter how her health failed, her ability to offer the true and honest account of how people lived their lives did not falter. She shows us Plumfield many years after with the boys grown to be men. There is a college there now, with Professor Bhaer as President, Meg as unofficial dean of women and Jo, as Mrs Bhaer, occupying much the same position in regard to the boys. Mr March is chaplain, Laurie and Amy are still general patrons and consultants. Thomas Niles appears in the background renamed Mr Tiber, just as Theodore Parker came into *Work* under the title of Mr Power.

All the Plumfield boys come back to have a talk, as they did of old, with Mother and Father Bhaer. The true heart of the story consists of Jo's conversations with each boy in turn, discussing with him what she has noticed of his weaknesses and his strengths, giving him good counsel as to how to go forward. Not much space is given to these deeply reaching interviews, nor are they in any sense dull preaching; they are merely most remarkable character study on the part of Jo, and behind her of Louisa Alcott. Dan has come home to Plumfield an almost unrecognizable wreck, but is welcomed, understood and given healing affection. He has been in prison, a year's sentence for shooting a man in a fit of blind rage. Mitigating circumstances have reduced the term, but when Louisa describes the dreadful suffering which confinement inflicts upon a wild free spirit like his, we see her still at the very height of her abilities. The prison chaplain, with endless patience, has managed to reach and touch the young man's inner sensibilities and gives him strength to endure until his sentence is completed. Most of the others are married or about to be and there is a general air of living-happily-ever-after about the whole scene. Louisa had no reason to think that this effort, almost her last, had fallen below the rest of her achievement.

A collection of stories for older but still young readers, called *A Garland for Girls*, was her last published book, coming not long before her death. Thus, as Louisa says at the end of *Jo's Boys*, 'the curtain falls for ever on the March family'. Time, however, has proved that this is not true and Louisa's family have lived long in public favour, showing that, in her contribution to literature for young people, the American family story has become an institution of which Louisa was one of the first, and by any standards, the greatest of exponents.

In her last summers she liked to go to a pleasant summer hotel on the slopes of an old friend, Mount Wachusett. From her window she could look down on the broad slopes, the winding river and the old house, Fruitlands, still standing, where she had first known what her life work was to be, the care of her family. There was no trace of bitterness in her heart as she sat there and thought of all that had come since then. She died in November 1888, fifty-six years old. She did not know that her father had gone two days before her. She did know that she had taken care of him to the very end.

PART TWO

The American
Family Story

VIII. Katy and Hildegarde

It is not surprising to find that Louisa Alcott's kind of books had predecessors. Only a very few of them achieved the quality of naturalness that *Little Women* presents. There is one piece of writing, however, which must in justice be mentioned as having the same characteristics, for the world should not forget, totally, the pleasant, friendly and alluring *Franconia Stories* (1850–53) of Jacob Abbott. His different vocations gave him a very wide and able interest in the minds of young people, an interest of which he made most earnest use. Born in 1803, he was a New Englander to the very heart and soul. He became, first, a professor of mathematics at Amherst, then an ordained Congregational minister, and finally a full-time writer for the young. He wrote more for their educational instruction than to purvey moral precepts as had so many who came before him. He set out to acquaint his readers with the events in the history of Europe which had so excited and stimulated him. He was a writer of unflagging industry and therefore added to this first enterprise a long series of biographies covering his subject thoroughly, beginning with Romulus and ending with Peter the Great. He became famous, however, chiefly for his Rollo books, wherein his young hero, in company with a well-informed uncle George, traversed the old world while Rollo learned history travelling through the places where it had all happened. 'In the intervals from more important work,' Abbott says apologetically, he wrote a sequence of small books depicting his own early life in a Maine village, with all the interests and pleasure of country living and all the small adventures of growing children, along with the larger events of the life of people working the land in the face of a far-from-friendly Nature.

Franconia is, in fact, a town in New Hampshire, but the country background is truly Maine with its forest-blanketed mountains, its plunging streams, its rocky and resistant soil and its indomitable people. The stories concern Phonny (short for Alphonso) with the aunt whom he visits, along with his cousins Malleville, Wallace and Stuyvesant. Phonny is, without a doubt, Jacob Abbott himself in his own young days. He has left word of himself as being 'of an impulsive temperament'. He and his hero seem both to have had a cheerful faculty for getting into endless scrapes, big and small and always unpredictable.

The chief factotum of Aunt Hanry's place is a French boy Beechnut (the children's version of the name of Antonio Bianchinette) whom Abbott rather injudiciously presents as being only twelve years old. But we forget this small error in our interest in him and his most original ways as the stories unfold. There are also the neighbours with whom these children consort, Caroline of the village with her small but forgivable vanities, Mary Bell who is such a support to her mother, Ellen Linn, living back in the mountains, all of them warmly natural and none of them too good. There is no moral pointed anywhere, but what we do gather from our acquaintance with them is that strong sense of responsibility, developing early as one of the traits necessary for meeting life in difficult surroundings. Somehow, amid the flood of his other books, Abbott's

Franconia Stories were submerged and, for the most part, forgotten. They have survived only here and there, a little set of small red volumes, descending from understanding parent to appreciative children and cherished as they truly deserve to be.

The *Rollo* books ushered in a long succession of accounts of travel written for young people. With the arrival of steam ocean-going vessels and greater facilities for travelling, more Americans were going abroad. There were the *Zigzag* journey books by Hezekiah Butterworth, rivalling the twelve volumes of Rollo, which were confined to Europe, by covering the larger part of the world in seventeen. The Knockabout Club, whose travels were recorded by Frederick Albion Ober, appeared to the world at much the same time. Amongst them all, however, the journeyings of the Bodley family described by Horace Scudder have been remembered the longest. This may be due to the fact that the central theme is the Bodley family itself and the reactions of the different children to the things and scenes to which they are introduced.

The series began with *The Doings of the Bodleys in Town and Country*, to be followed by *The Bodleys Telling Stories*, *The Bodleys on Wheels*, *The Bodleys Afoot*, and *The Bodleys Abroad*. Very much of the travel was in the United States; some of the small adventures, like the Bodleys themselves, are a trifle pedestrian, but our seeing them as individuals makes the narrative more than just one more travelogue. Mr Bodley, the father of Nathan, Philippa and Lucy, understands young people to their and our full satisfaction. He stops the carriage in which they are travelling to speak to some boys who are busy sailing boats in a roadside horse-trough. 'That's a nice little sloop of war that you have there,' he observes and the boys answer in kind by explaining that they are taking troops on board to set out in pursuit of pirates.

A second series takes up *The Bodley Grandchildren and Their Journey to Holland*, *The English Bodley Family* and *The Viking Bodleys* who visit Scandinavia. The books came out in handsome quarto volumes at Christmas time between the years 1875 and 1885.

The first author for whom we can trace a direct line of literary succession from Louisa Alcott was only three years younger than herself. She came of a definitely distinguished and learned family for she was three-times-great-grand-daughter of Jonathan Edwards, that fiery New England preacher and religious leader of his day. Her first years were spent in Cleveland, Ohio, but later her family moved to New Haven where her uncle was the President of Yale. She was not in any way an imitator of Louisa, although her books were in the same classification of American family story and they did much to establish on a permanent basis that area of writing for the young. One can say more: these two gifted women both followed the idea put forward by Thomas Niles that, as Louisa repeats, 'lively, simple books' are very much needed for young people. Susan Coolidge, whose real name was Sarah Chauncey Woolsey, was also a protégée of that observant publisher whose wise advice went far in giving his writers sensible guidance although he never seems to have interfered with their process of creation.

Susan's first book was a volume of short stories, entitled *The New-Year's Bargain*, based on the pleasant fancy of two children having made an agreement with the different months that each should tell them a story. She had so far published nothing but some verses in various magazines, but in the next year, 1872, she began her real literary career with *What Katy Did*. She herself was one of six children, and we find practically all of them depicted in this book and in the further chronicles of the Carr family. The central figure is Katy herself, the eldest, impatient, intense, impulsive, even sometimes defiant, but with many endearing qualities. In a moment of flagrant disobedience of authority she has a fall from a swing and is seriously injured, so that for weeks and months she cannot walk. Through it all she is surrounded by the spontaneous love and support of a loyal family which keep her from falling into real despair.

She could, in the ordinary course of nature, become hopelessly spoiled, making life difficult for everyone about her. But she is made of good stuff; she learns patience with great effort, she undertakes, on the death of her aunt, to oversee the family housekeeping from her wheeled chair, and after plenty of errors, she makes a real success of it. And with the whole process she comes to have a full and wise understanding of her brothers and sisters, so that, even though it may appear to be somewhat too precocious for anyone so young, it can well be accounted for by the severity of the ordeal through which she has come. There is no direct statement of this in the telling of the story; it is simply there to be observed as a truth.

Later, and possibly by Thomas Niles's suggestion, for he was very proud of her, she extended the Katy story into not merely a sequel but a series, something Louisa Alcott never felt herself prepared to do. *What Katy Did* (1872) was followed by *What Katy Did At School* (1873), *What Katy Did Next* (1886), *Clover* (1888) with Katy's younger sister as the principal heroine, and *In the High Valley* (1891). Thus a second worthy author came forward to offer books of force and originality to the developing theme of the American family story in children's literature. They were delightedly claimed by the readers for whom they were meant, who were beginning at last to have a chance to register their own tastes.

In considering the whole question one may ask whether it is necessary for a writer to belong to a large family to qualify as a successor to Louisa Alcott and Susan Coolidge. Laura E. Richards, who followed Susan Coolidge in this new and pleasant tradition, was equally blessed with abundance of personal material all about her. In her autobiography, *Stepping Westward*, she dedicates her book to her family, namely 'The Howes, the Gridleys, the Wards, the Cutlers, the Greenes, the Marions, the Gardiners and the Richardsons'. Her mother was Julia Ward Howe who wrote *The Battle Hymn of the Republic*. This first Julia was a famous beauty in her youth, *the* glamour girl of her social season, with suitors in quantity on every hand. She had, moreover, a glorious singing voice but she never used it professionally. Her final choice amongst the many who wished to marry her was someone a number of years older than herself, Dr Samuel Gridley Howe. He was a romantic figure in many eyes; for in his early years, when just graduated from the Harvard Medical School, he volunteered his services to the Greeks in their war of independence against Turkey. He had been stirred by the example of

Lord Byron who had done the same thing. When young
Dr Howe arrived in Greece, Byron had just died. His
effects were being distributed and Samuel brought back
to America Byron's helmet of steel inlaid with gold and
with a magnificently waving blue plume. Pursuing his
profession at home Dr Howe became deeply interested in
those who were physically afflicted, especially the deaf and
blind. His was the main spirit behind the founding of the
Perkins Institute for the Blind in Boston and the Massachusetts School for the Blind.

It was he who undertook the training of Laura Bridgeman,
a deaf and blind girl unable to talk because she never heard
spoken words, as was the case later with Helen Keller.
Samuel Howe brought her into a full and abundant life,
an accomplishment totally unheard of before. Charles
Dickens in his account of a visit to America gives large
space to the telling of what had been done for Laura
Bridgeman. Dr Howe's daughter was named after her, while
another daughter was the godchild and namesake of
Florence Nightingale. Miss Nightingale had become a
close friend and had come often to Samuel Howe when he
was in England, to ask his advice concerning her work in
the army hospitals. He had encouraged her warmly to go
forward in what she was doing, in spite of the disapproval
of her family and friends who thought that nursing soldiers
was no fit work for a lady.

The Howe family were greatly given to music. Julia
Ward Howe would gather her children about the piano
and they would sing together the songs in English, French,
German and Italian of which she knew so many. Laura
said afterwards that they all learned the rudiments of these

99

languages long before they approached them through the study of their grammar. With that sense of music in her head and heart, Laura was given to making all kinds of gay rhymes and bits of verse, mostly of humorous nonsense but most alluring to read and remember. She called it her hurdy-gurdy playing. Among her first published work were these rhymes, composed and illustrated mainly for *St Nicholas*, a new magazine then with its editor, Mary Mapes Dodge, becoming a cherished friend.

> 'A poor, unfortunate Hottentot,
> Was not content with his Lottentot.
> Quoth he, "For my dinner,
> As I am a sinner,
> There's nothing to put in the Pottentot!" '

is a sample of the kind and quality of these rhymes. Their most striking characteristic was their spontaneity, and they are apt to go on singing in one's own mind long after being read.

Laura was married to an architect, Henry Richards, in 1871. It was for her babies that she first made these verses and songs and sang them to small and encouraging listeners. A friend of Henry Richards, John Ames Mitchell, had just the right gifts for illustrating them, so that they were a great and always looked-for feature of *St Nicholas*.

The last of the Katy books was published in 1891 and here Susan Coolidge's series came to an end. The series, of course, gives an author more elbow room in the presenting of character, and furthering the reader's acquaintance with each member of a family. Louisa Alcott did not believe in sequels and presented them rather unwillingly, so that she never went on to the somewhat easier form of the series. But the American family story itself fell into the hands of a worthy successor to Susan Coolidge when Laura E. Richards began the Hildegarde books. In the first one, *Queen Hildegarde* (1889), the main figure is Hildegarde Graham who has no brothers or sisters. As the account goes on we have *Hildegarde's Holiday* and *Hildegarde's Home*, in which her mother, a cousin and a very dear friend all have important parts. But when we reach *Hildegarde's Neighbors* the family story comes into its own. Laura Richards reaches the highest level of her creative ability when she introduces us to the Merryweathers.

At the very opening of the book Hildegarde rushes to tell her mother the exciting news that a family is moving in next door, that she has stood behind the hedge and has seen them arrive—six children, large, medium and small, with cook, housemaid and seamstress, two dogs, two cats —'at least a basket mewed so I infer cats'—one canary bird and fourteen trunks. There is a pleasant, jovial father and a literary mother, somewhat on the absent-minded side, as Hildegarde notes, even on the first day since she arrives from the journey with a pen behind her ear.

Immediate acquaintance is made, for Hildegarde has really been needing friends although she has not consciously missed them. The Merryweathers are a gay, witty and keenly clever family, a truly notable addition to literature for young people. Mrs Richards had six children of her own and knew how to portray with accuracy Merryweathers of all ages and sizes. There is Bell, the same age as Hildegarde; there are the twin brothers of fifteen or sixteen (twins in other books always seem to be pictured as small). There are the youngsters and the elders. We see much taking place among the neighbours. We see the semi-elderly Colonel Ferrers, who, after an earlier, unhappy love affair, had retired to live as a morose and sombre recluse, now returning to what is evidently his younger and genial self. We see Hildegarde blossoming in the happiness of lively and congenial companionship. Towards the end of the book a new figure appears, a younger half brother of the Merryweathers' father, and we observe the beginnings of awakening romance. There is a further volume entitled *The Merryweathers*, and there are presently the Margaret books in another series, which is less remembered now since the Hildegarde books seem to have remained the favourites.

Laura Richards brought to her books a further feature for which we can be thankful. She was a great reader herself and knew well what would interest children in their reading. In almost all her writing she introduces, from time to time, references to her favourite passages, or her favourite books, just as Louisa Alcott could never resist presenting the occasions of home dramatics. Many a young reader of Mrs Richards's work has been intrigued by such a question as 'What was Marlowe's mighty line?' or by the casual mention of Robin Hood with pure delight arising from the mere sight of 'the good brown cover'. She was particularly attached to Scottish ballads and introduces us to many which we might not ordinarily have known.

During the depression of the eighteen-seventies, architecture became a profitless profession, so that the family moved to Gardinar, Maine, for Henry Richards to become the manager of the family paper mill. Laura rapidly became one of the moving spirits of the town, the head and front of all sorts of movements for civic betterment. Later she and her husband set up a summer camp for boys, the first in Maine, where one of the features of the daily programme was reading aloud, both in morning and evening. When seeking a name they chose 'Camp Merry-weather' after what was evidently Laura's favourite family.

She and her husband lived, both of them, to be over ninety years old and celebrated their seventieth wedding anniversary. In her eightieth year she was pressed by her publishers to produce another book of rhymes and jingles. At first she protested that she was too old, but presently consented to try and found that 'the old hurdy-gurdy' was grinding again. The book *Tirra Lirra*, was published in 1932. The Hildegarde series, with its last volume, *The Merryweathers*, covered the years 1889 to 1904. It was twenty-eight years later that *Tirra Lirra* appeared, with a few companion volumes of rhymes to follow up to 1939. They celebrated the fact that Laura had always found life to be an increasingly interesting and gay adventure.

IX. Polly, Nancy, Marguerite and Sally

Of all forms of writing for children the family story is perhaps the most difficult to write to order. One can set out with a full cast of characters and then find, as the work progresses, that the action focuses on one figure and the family element fades into unnecessary background. Or, on the other hand, one can imagine a story of one individual and then discover that it needs support and presently find that it has become a family story by necessity. This may account for the fact that the truly notable examples of the family story have not appeared in any continuous or chronological order. Their history leaves gaps here and there or sees them coming out together at certain periods of abundance.

The Five Little Peppers and How They Grew appeared in 1881 and was the beginning of an extended series. To consider it in such close succession to Laura Richards's Hildegarde and Merryweather volumes, it appears to be a somewhat sombre story, concerning difficult times and a family in which the children feel, although not too unhappily, the pressure of poverty that brings them close to real want. Through the eyes of Polly, the eldest girl, we look at a life that is indeed hard, yet not so much as to quench the earnest spirits of courageous children and a steadfast mother who is trying to support her family by sewing. During the course of the Peppers series the children grow up and we see them develop fully according to each one's earlier possibilities. The books go on to include

The Five Little Peppers Midway, *The Five Little Peppers Grown Up*, and *Phronsie Pepper*, the youngest girl, who, while she is still quite small, suddenly inherits an unexpected fortune. She uses it to found a school for orphans, which seems a violent departure from the easy naturalness of their growing up in the earlier stories.

As has been said, it may be some advantage for the writer of a family story to be a member of a large group of brothers and sisters and cousins, with the opportunity to use them all as models. But this Kate Douglas Smith (later Kate Douglas Wiggin), did not have, since her family consisted of one older sister and a very much younger half brother, with her mother and her stepfather whom she loved deeply. They were obliged, on account of her stepfather's health, to move to California, where her stepfather died just as she was beginning to grow up. At the school where she graduated, she had received a medal for elocution, a prize for French and another for English. This was a complete augury of the future, but for the moment she had no idea what her work in life was to be. Work she had to, for her stepfather's death left his little family not only penniless but burdened with debts.

Various people at different times had told her that she was 'a born teacher'. She had not thought much about this and had done nothing to make preparation for it. A friend, however, who was greatly interested in the new kindergarten educational system introduced by the German schoolmaster Froebel, persuaded Kate to take kindergarten training. The first person in America to adopt these new ideas was Elizabeth Peabody who had been Bronson Alcott's assistant at his school in Boston.

The fact of poverty did not in the least dismay the two sisters; they thought it was rather romantic than otherwise and they took it as a challenge. Kate did so well under training and proved herself so completely fitted for the new profession that she was almost at once, at the age of twenty-two, made the head of the Silver Street Kindergarten in the slums of San Francisco, the first such school west of the Rocky Mountains. She could understand children, she could play and sing for and with them; she was, besides, an instinctively good storyteller.

Her immediate success was remarkable both with the children and in the training of other teachers. After the first years and after her school had become justly famous, she travelled widely over the United States to visit other schools and to inspect the many experimental kindergartens being set up here and there. She spent some days at Concord, attending lectures at the new School of Philosophy, to hear Bronson Alcott and Emerson and Julia Ward Howe lecture. Louisa Alcott she did not see, for Louisa was evidently away at that time. She visited Hollis, Maine, where she had been born and there met the young lawyer, Samuel Bradley Wiggin, who came later to California where they were married in 1881. They had no children.

It was not long after her marriage that she and her husband moved to New York, although she went back to California frequently to visit her kindergarten and teachers' school which her sister Nora was carrying forward. To help finance this enterprise, which was so close to her heart, she wrote a little book *The Story of Patsy* which was published in paperback, her first entry into authorship. Later, moved by the spirit of Christmas, she wrote *The Birds' Christmas*

Carol. This had immediate and wide success, to her astonishment. In it she showed the little invalid, Carol, and the family of Ruggleses, just such a household as she must have seen often in her kindergarten teaching days. But since the main figure and this family were not really connected one cannot quite call this a family story.

Kate's brilliant young husband died very soon after their marriage, but she continued to live in New York. Writing had become her real profession but she was in demand everywhere, to lecture on kindergartens, to tell stories to school-children, to be beloved and lionized by devoted young readers. Meanwhile the list of her published works grew and to it was added, in 1902, *Rebecca of Sunnybrook Farm*. Rebecca is a real literary personality and was at once recognized as such in a wave of wild enthusiasm. Like *The Birds' Christmas Carol*, the book has been translated into many languages. It was made into a play and became the vehicle for the current movie star, Mary Pickford. The combination of the lively, volatile and resourceful Rebecca and her two old aunts, one totally misunderstanding her excitingly gifted young niece, the other sympathetic but too much under the domination of a masterful sister, makes a truly remarkable family story. It is also most truly and honestly an American one. Amongst all Mrs Wiggins's books it is only surpassed by *Mother Carey's Chickens*.

Older readers who love the book as well as the young ones, might be tempted to take Mrs Carey herself for the heroine, with her wise but sympathetic guidance of the family affairs, her patient and timely success in helping her young people to find the right way. But no younger reader could fail to see that it is Nancy who is the real heart of the story, that Nancy's radiant and friendly personality brings the whole into real life. The Careys, fallen upon financial misfortune, undertake to set up a new way of life in the little New England village of Beulah and undertake the rehabilitation of an old but charmingly alluring house. Their adjustment to the hard work and a new relation among them make for certain problems which true affection and common sense eventually solve. The little spoiled cousin, who is homeless yet taken in with all her faults upon her, is accepted into the real beauty of family living. The two Lord children, whose scientifically-absorbed father has allowed himself to become abominably selfish, have been allowed to grow up in shy and unhappy seclusion but are rescued by the sheer magnetism that a happy family exerts. Finally the young man who teaches them all in the village Academy finds reassurance and support in his efforts to prepare himself for the responsibilities and the opportunities of the world that lies before him. There is little doubt at the end that the Careys are going to know how to 'live happy ever after'.

Two writers who are poets as well as authors supremely destined for delighting children are Rachel Field and Elizabeth Coatsworth. With both of them it is difficult to decide which is the greater element in her work, the vividness of her prose or the magic feeling of her poetry. Rachel Field, who should have lived longer and given us more, had a capacity, especially in her poetry, for speaking the inmost thoughts of children as they would have spoken themselves if they had been able. The things that they notice, that they feel, that they think about, all these are voiced in what she has written. Here is a child in church:

'And when the little blacking smells,
And camphor balls and soap begin,
I do not have to look to know
That Mr Wells is coming in.'

Rachel Field herself, with her curly red hair, her warming, friendly smile was in herself a figure to be long cherished in memory. Her apartment in Greenwich Village in New York was a place where all young people, struggling to make their way in a great city, were so generously welcomed that they went away reassured and full of hope. Her books, including her novels and her stories for younger people, are always rich in detail of time and place and personality as well as vibrating with life. Her *Hitty: Her First Hundred Years* celebrates the indestructibility of a small wooden doll and her manifold adventures in the course of outliving several generations of more frail human beings.

Rachel Field's *Calico Bush* is the story of a French girl, Marguerite Ledoux, who is 'bound out' as was the custom of the time for someone who had no family or means of support. She is to work until she is eighteen in a family that is just setting out to make a new home on an island off the shores of Mount Desert, on the coast of New England. The story is illuminating, absorbing and, in certain parts, breathless. A pioneering theme is almost certain to lead to a family story, since all the members are obliged to act together in the struggle to make the new life that they are seeking. The 'calico bush' is the pink-flowered mountain laurel, which suggests and represents New England as no other flower can do. There is an old ballad about the calico bush which haunts with its measures the

fortunes of those in the story. Marguerite and her grandmother are crossing from France, bound for Canada, when
the ship lands at Marblehead and her grandmother dies
almost immediately of an illness contracted on board,
leaving Marguerite penniless and alone. It is the village
law that anyone so situated must be 'bound out' to work
for a family for a term of years in return for her support.
She is thirteen years old when she sets out with the Sargent
family for their journey up the coast to their new home.
Marguerite can speak English but not as the others do,
and for this the eldest Sargent boy teases her unmercifully
as she takes care of the smaller children.

It is true that she is not like the others: she is made of
finer stuff, firmer of courage, quicker of wit in an emergency, as time proves. We learn to know each member of
the family and the few neighbours, for all must hold
together in their resistance to storm and cold in winter and
the threat of Indian raids when harsh Nature is gentle
again. In the end they establish a safe home and Marguerite,
although she is given a chance to leave, stays with them to
be part of the growing settlement. We see before the story
is over that Marguerite is the saving grace of that first
expedition and that her children will be, in time, of that
descent of which Rachel Field speaks in her poem at the
beginning of the book.

> 'It's years now since they were broken and lost,
>   Sturdier stock has weathered the frost,
>   But here and there in some far place
>   A name persists and a foreign face,
>   A lift of shoulder, a turn of the head;
>   Along with an Old World chest or bed;

A Breton Bible, a silver spoon;
And feet more quick to a fiddle tune;
A gift for taking the last, mad chance
Because some great-great came from France.'

The story that Elizabeth Coatsworth has to tell pertains
to pioneers also and must be mentioned here because it is
so original and so enchantingly told. In *Away Goes Sally*
we have another child without brothers or sisters or parents,
her family being three devoted aunts and two uncles, all
living on one of the rock-ribbed farms of northern Massachusetts. At the head of the family is Uncle Joseph who,
but for one other, is the leader and master of the household.
The one other is Aunt Nannie, the eldest of the three
sisters, practical as to all domestic matters and firmly
obstinate in keeping to all customary ways. There is
younger Aunt Deborah, and younger still and prettier is
Aunt Esther. And besides there is Uncle Eben who, unlike
the others, is fat and lazy and always enjoys life. And there
is Sally, small, eager, black-eyed, whom they all love
deeply and who, in turn, adores them all and would never
think of questioning their decisions or their orders.

Uncle Joseph has a letter from a cousin who has moved
further north to the still scarcely-settled valley of the
Penobscot, in ideal farming land. He urges them all to pull
up stakes on their worn-out farm and come to settle there.
Uncle Joseph wants to go but Aunt Nannie flatly refuses.
She will live and die in her own house where she was
born, will sit by her own fire and sleep in her own bed.
Nothing is to move her.

Sally discerns, as children do, that Uncle Joseph still has
the project in mind and she also guesses that Aunt Nannie

is weakening, though still keeping up a stout front of refusal. Finally Uncle Joseph develops a plan and suddenly, when winter has partly gone by, he and his helpers appear from the woods where they have been building a little log house on runners, complete with windows and Franklin stove and chimney, with two rooms inside and beds enough for them all, even to a basket for Dinah, the black cat. Aunt Nannie can go north, still sitting at her own fireside and sleeping in her own bed. She yields gracefully and, with six yoke of oxen to draw them, they set out northward.

It takes all the ability and staying power of the whole household to make that journey through sleet and storm, across frozen rivers, through dark forests and past lonely cabins. With her delicate and poetic skill, Elizabeth Coatsworth makes the reader aware, almost imperceptibly, how beautiful was that journey, in spite of its hardships and dangers. We see it all through the eyes of Sally, who drinks in all the beauty and wonder with every breath. Spring is very close as they all stand at last on the slope above the valley of the Penobscot, and see how fair is the landscape that spreads out at their feet. The open land is growing green and the distant mountains are as blue as the sky.

' "Can we really own this?" Aunt Nannie asks wonderingly as she stands by her brother on the hillside.

"Yes," replies Uncle Joseph. "We can own as far as you can see." '

This is to be Sally's home, and Elizabeth describes it thus:

'The wind will go running down the wheat
And men and beasts will have food to eat;
And a child who is wandering all alone
May find mushrooms as round as a wave-worn stone,

Or gather strawberries round and red;
Or glimpse a deer with an antlered head;
Or leaning against the pasture bars
May stare toward the west at the early stars.
All, all awaits. Up hill, down valley,
The time is ripe and away goes Sally.'

x. Two Boys, Lucinda and Laura

This study cannot be a definitive record of the American family story. What is given is merely a sampling of some of the best representatives of this class of writing for children, the whole idea stemming from Louisa Alcott's original example. The books which are described here are chosen as those which seem to have contributed most to establishing a new tradition, that of presenting family life as it is lived. Fundamentally their authors stand for the same things as Charlotte Yonge, Julia Horatio Ewing and Mrs Molesworth, whose books were read eagerly by American children during much the same periods. The American stories, however, compared with the British, have such very different backgrounds and present, in so many cases, more varied ways of life.

It is probably already obvious that, in the examples so far given, this form of literary art has been written always by women for the reading of girls. This is only reasonable, since for women family life is a primary responsibility, and for girls a picture of the future of which they dream. Theirs, they know, will be the largest and most significant contribution to the family life in which they see themselves taking part. But it is not invariably true as we see when we look a little closer. We may take two examples of books about boys, written by men (and eagerly read by girls), which came out in different generations but are still more or less akin, certainly in the fact that they are decidedly family stories: Thomas Bailey Aldrich's *Story of a Bad Boy* (1870) and Booth Tarkington's *Penrod* (1914).

Tom Bailey—'not such a very bad boy' as the author says at the start and with which we readily agree—has as guides and guardians a most understanding uncle and aunt, who, although they are in their elderly years, accept him happily with all the vagaries of teenage boys and are neither shocked nor alarmed by the various kinds of small troubles into which he falls. They are quietly comforting when he and his mates lose their little friend Binny Wallace in a tragic accident; they give him support and reassurance when he loses his father in far-off New Orleans.

There is also a very pretty grown-up cousin with whom Tom thinks he has fallen in love, on whose account he becomes a Blighted Being. The story very happily reproduces the life in Rivermouth, which is actually Portsmouth, New Hampshire, one of that State's few seaports. One sees the old decaying warehouses along the water-front where a faint scent of spices and coffee, 'the ghost of the old East India trade', still gives a reminder of the town's more prosperous years.

None of this serenity of living appears in the chronicle of Penrod. His father and mother and sisters all love him dearly, but are completely baffled by him and by the various phases through which he goes. They do not understand him in the least, nor does Penrod have any real inkling of what they actually want of him and thus falls into all manner of cheerful trouble. His mother and sister laboriously prepare him for the *Children's Pageant of the Table Round*, written by Mrs Lora Rewbush. She does not specify to the parents just what the costumes are to be, as long as they are 'medieval and as artistic as possible'. He is to speak the lines:

> 'I hight Sir Launcelot du Lake, the child,
> Gentle-hearted, meek and mild.
> I do my share, though but a tot—
> I pray you knight Sir Launcelot.'

For this he is dressed in a pair of his sister's long stockings to be hopefully regarded as tights, and in one of his mother's discarded blouses as a tunic. Worst of all, he is equipped with a pair of trunks manufactured from his father's very recognizable red flannel underwear. He knows he cannot bring himself to appear before his young contemporaries in this guise, to be an object of derision, so, as the opportunity suddenly presents itself, he borrows the school janitor's very ample blue overalls and appears in them. He brings down the house but not in the manner that the earnest authoress of the *Children's Pageant of the Table Round* had intended. He is roundly punished for his action although it was truly no more than an effort of self-defence. It is only one more moment in his bewilderment as to what is to be violently condemned or what is to be taken as earnestly commendable. There is no sense of tragedy or bitterness in his outlook. It is mere wonder at life being so very puzzling. There is a bit of symbolism at the end, which Penrod readily understands. His great-aunt Sarah, on his twelfth birthday, gives him a very ancient sling-shot which he is to deliver to his father. 'Tell him', her message runs, 'that I took it away from him thirty-five years ago when he had killed my best hen—accidentally. I believe I can trust him with it now.'

The depth and richness of the background out of which Ruth Sawyer composes her stories is perhaps not strictly evident in the book with which we are concerned here. She is not only a gifted story-teller in the highest sense but she is a scholar of folklore and legend. In her own person she has explored to the depths the native tales of Ireland and Spain, and she draws from them the most dramatic force and effect when she gives them orally. No one who has ever heard her give one of her story-telling sessions can lose the memory of a moving and thrilling experience.

Her distinctly family story, *The Year of Jubilo* (1940), offers the picture of a family embattled, making its own way against the difficult circumstances of our complicated modern life. It shows a somewhat similar situation to that in *Mother Carey's Chickens*—and it is indeed a frequent one in ordinary life. In this case the complications of re-adjustment are a good deal greater, and it is the children who turn to helping their mother, a frail little person upon whom misfortune has fallen. All five children set about doing his or her best manfully to uphold her.

The whole action is seen from the point of view of Lucinda, a volatile and appealing person whom we have already learned to know in a previous book, *Roller Skates*. This girl is the youngest of the family, with a next older brother who has a positive genius for teasing and cannot help exercising it at Lucinda's expense, tempted thereto by her satisfactorily explosive temper.

The real leader of the family is Douglas, the eldest son, who is a calming and comforting support to Lucinda in her efforts, at fourteen, to learn to cook for the household while her brothers set to work to earn the family living by fishing for lobsters and taking any other opportunity available. Her brother Carter never misses a chance of deriding her failures, a practice which she finally learns to endure in smouldering silence since otherwise it so deeply disturbs the family harmony. The scene of the story is a remote New England seashore village, where they have formerly spent only the summers in carefree vacations. But Lucinda loves it all, and finds solace in the freedom of thought and action, in the beautiful surroundings of sand and sea, the delight in unusual and inappropriate friendships with all sorts and kinds of individuals. To become acquainted with Lucinda, with her romantic longings, her impatience and her all-embracing good-will towards life is something for which to be thankful. The book is frankly autobiographical, with Lucinda as Ruth Sawyer's self, as is fully admitted. It is a subtle art to be able to write about oneself without a trace of vanity and yet to make that person enticing and endearing. It is a gift which Ruth Sawyer exercises to the full.

The light-hearted Moffats make up a family which always seems to be having a delightful time, simply because they find just living and finding out new things by experiment a most enjoyable experience. Eleanor Estes in her series, *The Moffats* (1941), *The Middle Moffat* (1942) and *Rufus M.* (1943), has made good use of the series device to give an extraordinarily happy picture of American family life. It seems as though we get closer to Jane as the middle Moffat, than to the others. When Mrs Estes read her paper before the American Library Association on the occasion of her receiving the Newbery Medal she spoke particularly of 'the lamb chop chapter' as though this was one of her favourite incidents.

It presents Jane, the middle Moffat, in the exacting position of dining out in the house of people whom she does not know well and of not being certain of the procedure when formal waiting on the table is in order. If there is only one chop left on the platter, who should take it? Jane has been instructed in one school of thought that the last chop is destined for the maid in the kitchen so that it is the part of good manners to leave it there. She is offered the platter with one chop on it; just what is she meant to do? While she hesitates in agony of doubt, the mistress of the house at the head of the table says to the maid: 'Olga, I don't know what kind of manners Janey will think that we have. Not to serve Janey her chop before Nancy and Beatrice.' 'Oh, that's all right,' exclaims Janey in a vast rush of relief, 'I knew it was for me!' She has learned in that desperate moment that other families have other ways and that to learn what they are is part of learning the art of living. One always feels more cheerful about everything after reading a Moffat book.

After we have once been made acquainted with one of Elizabeth Enright's families, we feel that they have been personal friends of ours for a long time and will continue to be so for a longer one. In her account of the Melendy children in her book *The Saturdays* (1941) she accomplishes this full development of individual characters in one book instead of embracing the advantages of a series.

The Melendy family is ingenious as well as attractive. They found the Independent Saturday Afternoon Adventure Club (code name Isaac) with four members. Three of them have an allowance of fifty cents a week. If they agree to 'pool their resources' there will then be the rather magnificent sum total of $1.50 which each can use in turn. The smallest of the family, Oliver, is not eligible, especially since his allowance is only ten cents a week. But he makes loud protests, promises to combine his ten cents with the family fund and so is provisionally accepted. The choices are to be for something really worth having or doing, and they are varied, and wholly satisfying, a picture gallery, a grand opera, a visit to a beauty shop. Oliver, collecting his final total, manages to slip away unnoticed and goes to the circus, to his great enjoyment, but loses himself on the way home. Thanks to the very efficient and kindly police force of New York City he returns riding on the saddle in front of a mounted policeman, with all his troubles vanished in the glory of such an arrival.

Perhaps the fullest measure of the possibilities of the American family story has been realized in the pioneer chronicle, written in an extended series, by Laura Ingalls Wilder. The adventures are along the western frontier, as it moves steadily further and further from its beginnings, progressing so fast that even a single childhood can see a large measure of change. All the possibilities of a thrilling life in new and unsettled country are made the most of, just as it is experienced by a family of six children, an untiringly courageous mother and an ever-restless father in whom the pioneering spirit reigns supreme.

The story begins in the first volume with *Little House in the Big Woods* (1932), when Laura, from whose point of view the whole tale is told, is five years old. She grows up gradually in *Little House on the Prairie*, *On the Banks of Plum Creek*, *By the Shores of Silver Lake*. *The Long Winter* and *Little Town on the Prairie*.

The separate account, *Farmer Boy*, tells the story of Almanzo Wilder whom Laura later marries. The record is of Laura Ingalls herself, her parents and three sisters. She has not changed even the names. The happenings were all there, but the telling of them is what makes the real story, the sense of the wide spaces, the snow and furious winds, the long hot dry days of summer, the pressure of cold and hunger in winter, the rich plenty of harvest —and all the people who have had part in living with them and through them. In the whole of the account we see that indomitable spirit with which a father and his family move undaunted from place to place, setting up a family stronghold against the terrors and hardships of pioneer life, then when civilization begins to crowd in even to the smallest extent, pulling up stakes and, in bold spirit, doing it all over again in a new environment. It was thus that the whole country of the U.S.A. was finally brought under the plough, under neighbourly settlement, with the establishment of schools and churches and a rough-hewn political organization and the peaceful order of a wide new land. The sources from which an account can be drawn, from its wide prairies, its forests, its streams and mountains, its scattered villages turning so quickly into growing cities, its varied people and its always present and always individual children are inexhaustible. It is exciting and absorbing to speculate whither the American family story will turn next. One can always be sure that if it is real, it will truly record the spirit and the heart of the story of America itself.

Bibliography

I. LOUISA M. ALCOTT

Flower Fables. Boston, George W. Briggs and Company, 1855.

Hospital Sketches. Boston, James Redpath, 1863.

Hospital Sketches and Camp and Fireside Stories. Boston, Roberts Brothers, 1869. London, Sampson Low and Company, 1870.

On Picket Duty, and Other Tales. Boston, James Redpath, 1864.

Moods. Boston, Loring, 1865. London, G. Routledge and Sons, 1866.

Morning-Glories, and Other Stories. Boston, H. B. Fuller, 1868.

Kitty's Class-Day. Boston, Loring, 1868.

Three Proverb Stories. Boston, Loring, 1868.

Little Women or, Meg, Jo, Beth and Amy. Boston, Roberts Brothers, 1868. Published with a second part, Roberts Brothers, 1869. London, Sampson Low and Company, 1871. (Part II was subsequently published in London as a separate volume under a variety of titles, and is generally known today as *Good Wives.*)

An Old-Fashioned Girl. Boston, Roberts Brothers, 1870. London, Sampson Low and Company, 1870.

Little Men: Life at Plumfield with Jo's Boys. Boston, Roberts Brothers, 1871. London, Sampson Low and Company, 1871.

My Boys. Volume I of *Aunt Jo's Scrap-Bag.* Boston, Roberts Brothers, 1872. London, Sampson Low and Company, 1872.

Shawl-Straps. Volume II of *Aunt Jo's Scrap-Bag.* Boston, Roberts Brothers, 1872. London, Sampson Low and Company, 1873.

Work: A Story of Experience. Boston, Roberts Brothers, 1873. London, Sampson Low and Company, 1873.

Cupid and Chow-Chow. Volume III of *Aunt Jo's Scrap-Bag.* Boston, Roberts Brothers, 1874. London, Sampson Low and Company, 1873.

Eight Cousins; or, The Aunt-Hill. Boston, Roberts Brothers, 1875. London, Sampson Low and Company, 1875.

Silver Pitchers: and Independence, a Centennial Love Story. Contains 'Transcendental Wild Oats.' Boston, Roberts Brothers, 1876. London, Sampson Low and Company, 1876.

Rose in Bloom. Boston, Roberts Brothers, 1876. London, Sampson Low and Company, 1877.

A Modern Mephistopheles. Boston, Roberts Brothers, 1877. Reprinted with 'A Whisper in the Dark', 1889.

Under the Lilacs. Boston, Roberts Brothers, 1878. London, Sampson Low and Company, 1877.

My Girls. Volume IV of *Aunt Jo's Scrap-Bag.* Boston, Roberts Brothers, 1878.

Jimmy's Cruise in the Pinafore. Volume V of *Aunt Jo's Scrap-Bag.* Boston, Roberts Roberts, 1879. London, Sampson Low and Company, 1879.

Jack and Jill. A Village Story. Boston, Roberts Brothers, 1880. London, Sampson Low and Company, 1880.

Proverb Stories. Boston, Roberts Brothers, 1882. London, Sampson Low and Company, 1882.

An Old-Fashioned Thanksgiving. Volume VI of *Aunt Jo's Scrap-Bag.* Boston, Roberts Brothers, 1882. London, Sampson Low and Company, 1882.

Spinning-Wheel Stories. Boston, Roberts Brothers, 1884. London, Sampson Low and Company, 1884.

Lulu's Library. Volume I. Boston, Roberts Brothers, 1886. London, Sampson Low and Company, 1886.

Lulu's Library. Volume II. Reprint of *Flower Fables*, with some additions. Boston, Roberts Brothers, 1887.

Lulu's Library. Volume III. Boston, Roberts Brothers, 1889.

Jo's Boys and How They Turned Out. Boston, Roberts Brothers, 1886. London, Sampson Low and Company, 1886.

A Garland for Girls. Boston, Roberts Brothers, 1888. London, Blackie and Son, 1888.

Comic Tragedies. Written by 'Jo' and 'Meg' and Acted by the 'Little Women'. Boston, Roberts Brothers, 1893. London, Sampson Low and Company, 1893.

Thoreau's Flute. 3 pages. Reprint from the *Atlantic Monthly.* Detroit, The Stylus Press, 1899.

Three Unpublished Poems. Fruitlands Collection. Boston, Clara Endicott Sears, 1919.

II. THE AMERICAN FAMILY STORY

Jacob Abbott. *The Franconia Stories.* New York, Harper and Brothers, 1850-53. London, *Agnes, Caroline* and *Stuyvesant,* Ward and Company, 1853; *Rodolphus,* Thomas Allman, 1852; *Beechnut, Ellen Linn, Malleville, Mary Bell, Mary Erskine* and *Wallace,* Thomas Allman, 1853.

Horace Scudder. *The Bodley Family.* Eight volumes. Boston, Hurd and Houghton Mifflin, 1875-1885.

Susan Coolidge (Sarah Chauncey Woolsey). *What Katy Did.* Boston, Roberts Brothers, 1872. London, Ward Lock and Tyler, 1873.

What Katy Did at School. Boston, Roberts Brothers, 1873. London, Ward Lock and Tyler, 1874.

What Katy Did Next. Boston, Roberts Brothers, 1886. London, Ward Lock and Tyler, 1887.

Clover. Boston, Roberts Brothers, 1888. London and Glasgow, Blackie and Son, 1958.

In the High Valley. Boston, Roberts Brothers, 1891. London, and Glasgow, Blackie and Son, 1959.

Laura E. Richards. *Queen Hildegarde.* Boston, Estes and Lauriat, 1889. London, Gay and Bird, 1889.

Hildegarde's Holiday, Boston, Estes and Lauriat, 1891. London, Gay and Bird, 1891.

Hildegarde's Home. Boston, Estes and Lauriat, 1892.

Hildegarde's Neighbors. Boston, Estes and Lauriat, 1895.

The Merryweathers. Boston, Estes and Lauriat, 1904.

Tirra Lirra. Boston, Little Brown, 1932. London, G. G. Harrap and Company, 1933.

Margaret Sidney (Harriet Mulford Lothrop). *The Five Little Peppers and How They Grew.* Boston, D. Lothrop Company, 1881. London, Hodder and Stoughton, 1881.

The Five Little Peppers Midway. Boston, D. Lothrop Company, 1893. London, T. Fisher Unwin, 1909.
The Five Little Peppers Grown Up. Boston, D. Lothrop Company, 1892.
Phronsie Pepper. Boston, D. Lothrop Company, 1897.
Kate Douglas Wiggin. *The Story of Patsy*. Boston, Houghton Mifflin, 1883. London, Gay and Bird, 1889.
The Birds' Christmas Carol. Boston, Houghton Mifflin, 1887. London, Gay and Bird, 1891.
Rebecca of Sunnybrook Farm. Boston, Houghton Mifflin, 1902. London, Gay and Bird, 1903.
Mother Carey's Chickens. New York, Grosset and Dunlap, 1911. London Hodder and Stoughton, 1911.
Rachel Field. *Hitty*. New York, Macmillan, 1929. London, G. Routledge and Sons, 1932.
Calico Bush. New York, Macmillan, 1934.
Elizabeth Coatsworth. *Away Goes Sally*. New York, Macmillan, 1934. London, Henry Woodfield, 1955.
Thomas Bailey Aldrich. *Story of a Bad Boy*. Boston, Fields Osgood and Company, 1870. London, Sampson Low and Company, 1870.
Booth Tarkington, *Penrod*. New York, Doubleday, Page and Company, 1914. London, Hodder and Stoughton, 1914.
Ruth Sawyer. *The Year of Jubilo*. New York, Viking, 1940. (as *Lucinda's Year of Jubilo*) London, Bodley Head, 1965.
Eleanor Estes. *The Moffats*. New York, Harcourt, Brace and World, 1941. London, Bodley Head, 1959.
The Middle Moffat. New York, Harcourt, Brace and World, 1942. London, Bodley Head, 1960.
Rufus M. New York, Harcourt, Brace and World, 1943. London, Bodley Head, 1960.
Elizabeth Enright. *The Saturdays*. New York, Holt, Rinehart, 1941. London, William Heinemann, 1955.
Laura Ingalls Wilder. *Little House in the Big Woods*. Eight volumes. New York, Harper and Brothers, 1932-43. London, *Little House in the Big Woods*, Methuen, 1956; *Little House on the Prairie*, 1957; *On the Banks of Plum Creek*,

Methuen, 1958; *By the Shores of Silver Lake*, Lutterworth
Press, 1961; *The Long Winter*, Lutterworth Press, 1962; *Little
Town on the Prairie*, 1963; *These Happy Golden Years*, Lutter-
worth Press, 1964; *Farmer Boy*, Lutterworth Press, 1965.